Lydia Fotheringham is based in Perth where she maintains a strong base of farming clients. A solicitor with 29 years' experience she is accredited by the Law Society of Scotland as a Specialist in Agricultural Law. Lydia is described in Chambers 2020 as "pragmatic and sensible in her approach."

A Practical Introduction to Scottish Agricultural Law

Second Edition

A Practical Introduction to Scottish Agricultural Law

Second Edition

Lydia M Fotheringham

LLB (Hons), Dip LP, TEP

Accredited by the Law Society of Scotland
as a Specialist in Agricultural Law

Solicitor, Anderson Beaton Lamond

Law Brief Publishing

Published 2025 by Law Brief Publishing, an imprint of Law Brief Publishing Ltd
30 The Parks
Minehead
Somerset
TA24 8BT

www.lawbriefpublishing.com

Paperback: 978-1-916698-69-7

This book is dedicated to Alan and Archie

without whose love and support it

would not have been possible.

PREFACE

Thanks to my colleagues past and present who have supported my interest in agricultural law and given me the time to write this book. Thanks to my family for their patience. Thanks also to Tim Kevan and Garry Wright for suggesting the first edition of this book and helping me through the writing process of both editions.

The law as stated is believed to be correct as at 30th November 2024.

Lydia Fotheringham
November 2024

CONTENTS

CHAPTER ONE

INTRODUCTION AND STATUTORY FRAMEWORK

This book is intended as a simple, introductory guide to agricultural law in Scotland.

I have concentrated on those areas encountered most frequently in practice which I hope will be of assistance to law students, solicitors engaged in other areas of practice with an interest in agricultural law and other professionals such as land agents and accountants.

My intention has been to provide the reader with a guide to the legislative framework which has been under almost constant review during the last 20 years. It would be impossible within such a short text to include details of the history of these provisions or the body of case law interpreting them for which reference should be made to other more detailed works.

As secure 1991 Act tenancies become less common in practice Tenants of these types of tenancy are at risk of being as over-burdened with legislation as Crofters. I have tried to balance comment on 1991 Act tenancies, which remains relevant, with coverage of the new forms of tenancy which are gradually becoming more accepted.

References in this book are to:-

- The Agricultural Holdings (Scotland) Act 1991 (the 1991 Act)
- The Agricultural Holdings (Scotland) Act 2003 (the 2003 Act)

- The Land Reform (Scotland) Act 2016 (the 2016 Act)
- The Land Reform (Scotland) Bill 2024 (the 2024 Bill)

The Law is as stated at 30th November 2024.

CHAPTER TWO

1991 ACT TENANCIES

The expression "1991 Act tenancy" applies to a range of agricultural tenancies created in a variety of circumstances. Many of these tenancies came into effect long before the enactment of the 1991 Act.

This chapter discusses the defining characteristics of such tenancies and the various ways in which they can be created.

If any lease is to be valid in Scotland there must be agreement on :-

- who are the parties to the lease
- what property is subject to the lease
- the rent payable and
- the duration.

All four of these elements must be present before an agricultural lease of any kind can be created. It is worth bearing in mind that rent need not be paid in cash and it is possible to argue that services rendered or any other kind of non-cash payment form a "consideration" equivalent to rent.

An agricultural lease need not be in writing and whereas an unwritten lease would not be binding on successors in the general law, agricultural leases enjoy the protection of the 1991 Act.

The Act applies to agricultural holdings which are defined as the aggregate of agricultural land comprised in any lease which is not related to the tenant's continuation in any office, appointment or employment held under the Landlord.

Agricultural land is defined as land used for agriculture for the purposes of a trade or business. This is an important distinction and means that land used for the rearing of animals kept as pets can never create an agricultural tenancy. The definition refers to the agricultural use being for the purpose of a trade or business but there is no requirement for the trade or business to be run to any particularly high standard nor indeed to be profitable.

S3 of the 1991 Act creates the element of security of tenure which is the hallmark of a 1991 Act tenancy. The tenancy of an agricultural holding does not end at the termination date but continues by tacit relocation for another year after the stated termination date and from year to year thereafter unless the Landlord has served a notice to quit or the Tenant has served a notice of intention to quit.

The circumstances in which the Landlord can serve an incontestable notice to quit are extremely limited, see Chapter 15. The right of the tenant to bequeath the tenancy or the right of the executors of a deceased tenant to nominate an acquirer on intestacy mean that this security of tenure can continue through many generations of the Tenant's family.

There are a number of ways in which 1991 Act tenancies can be created. The law prior to the enactment of the 2003 Act is still relevant to the vast majority of 1991 Act tenancies in existence.

Before the enactment of the 2003 Act, a 1991 Act tenancy could be created in some of the following ways. This is not an exhaustive list –

- The Landlord and the Tenant intended the 1991 Act to apply to the lease and entered into a written lease after the 1991 Act came into force.

- The Landlord and the Tenant entered into a lease which was governed by the legislation prior to the 1991 Act, but the 1991 Act now applies to that lease

- The Landlord leased an agricultural holding to a Tenant prior to 27th November 2003 but there was no written lease

- The Landlord and the Tenant entered into a lease of grazing land and, prior to 27th November 2003, the Tenant's actings took the arrangement outwith the limited scope of the now repealed s2 of the 1991 Act. This could be for example by the Tenant growing a crop on the land or staying in occupation for more than 364 days. A 1991 Act tenancy would thereby be created by default.

Following enactment of the 2003 Act, 1991 Act tenancies can only be created under s1 of the 2003 Act which contains two main provisions –

- any new 1991 Act tenancies entered into must be in writing and

- must state that the 1991 Act applies to the tenancy.

These provisions mean it is no longer possible for a 1991 Act tenancy to be created where there is an unwritten lease or a failed grazing lease. In both of these scenarios the default position is now the creation of a Short Limited Duration Tenancy (see chapter 3) because a 1991 Act tenancy must be in writing and state that the 1991 Act applies.

S1 of the 2003 Act goes on to state that the tenancy of an agricultural holding entered into before 27th November 2003 to which the 1991

Act applied was henceforth to be known as a 1991 Act tenancy, regardless of the date when the lease was entered into

There are now fewer than 5,000 1991 Act tenancies in Scotland.

CHAPTER THREE

LEASES – 2003 ACT

The 2003 Act, as now amended by the 2016 Act, introduced a range of new types of agricultural tenancy. The intention was to encourage Landlords to make land available to rent using the new forms of tenancy which have fixed durations.

Short Limited Duration Tenancies

A Short Limited Duration Tenancy (SLDT) is a lease of land for a period of 5 years or less which is not a grazing lease, a 1991 Act tenancy or a let of land to a tenant while the tenant continues in any office, appointment or employment held under the Landlord.

If a grazing tenant remains in occupation of the grazing land following the termination date of the grazing lease with the consent of the Landlord then the original grazing lease converts to an SLDT for 5 years or such shorter period as the Landlord and the Tenant may agree. Before the 2003 Act came into force a Landlord who allowed a grazing Tenant to remain in occupation after the expiry of the grazing lease risked creating a 1991 Act tenancy.

If an SLDT is for a period of less than 5 years and the Tenant continues in occupation after the expiry of the term of the lease with the consent of the Landlord then the tenancy continues to have effect as if it were for a term of 5 years or such shorter period as the Landlord and the Tenant may agree.

If an SLDT is for a period of 5 years and the Tenant remains in occupation after the expiry of the term of the lease with the consent of the Landlord the lease becomes an MLDT (formerly an LDT) for ten years commencing on the start date of the original SLDT.

Where an SLDT has ended by agreement or expired without the Tenant remaining in occupation and the Landlord and the Tenant want to enter into a new SLDT of the same land the duration of the first let is added to the duration of the new let and if together the total period of let is more than 5 years then the lease becomes a Modern Limited Duration Tenancy under s5A(4) of the 2016 Act.

Limited Duration Tenancies

Limited Duration Tenancies (LDTs) were introduced by the 2003 Act but abolished by the 2016 Act.

No new LDTs can be created but those already in place remain in effect.

When the 2003 Act first came into force an LDT was for a minimum of 15 years. This was reduced to 10 years in 2011. There was no maximum duration for an LDT.

An LDT was defined as a lease of agricultural land for a period of at least 10 years which was not a 1991 Act tenancy or a let of land to a Tenant while the Tenant continues in any office, appointment or employment held under the Landlord.

An LDT could arise either by agreement between the parties to enter into an LDT or by default in various circumstances. An LDT for 10 years, commencing on the start date of the SLDT or other purported arrangement, was created:-

- if parties attempted to enter into a lease of agricultural land for a period of more than 5 but less than 10 years

- if during the course of an SLDT the Landlord and the Tenant agreed in writing to convert the lease to an LDT

- if the Tenant remained in occupation of the land at the expiry of an SLDT and the Landlord consented

- if, as above, an SLDT has ended by agreement or expired without the Tenant remaining in occupation and the Landlord and the Tenant wished to enter into a new SLDT of the same land, the duration of the first let was added to the duration of the new let and the total period of let was more than 5 years

- the Landlord and the Tenant of a 1991 Act tenancy agreed under s2 of the 2003 Act to terminate the 1991 Act tenancy and substitute it with an LDT

Modern Limited Duration Tenancies

Modern Limited Duration Tenancies (MLDTs) were introduced by the 2016 Act as a replacement for LDTs.

A Modern Limited Duration Tenancy is a lease of agricultural land for a period of at least 10 years which is not a 1991 Act tenancy or a let of land to a Tenant while the Tenant continues in any office, appointment or employment held under the Landlord.

As with LDTs there are various circumstances in which an MLDT can arise These are:

- the Landlord and the Tenant agree to enter into an MLDT in writing

- the Landlord and the Tenant attempt to enter into a lease of agricultural land for a period of more than 5 but less than 10 years

- if, during the course of an SLDT, the Landlord and the Tenant agree in writing to convert the lease to an MLDT

- if the Tenant remained in occupation of the land at the expiry of an SLDT and the Landlord consents

- if, as above, an SLDT has ended by agreement or expires without the Tenant remaining in occupation and the Landlord and the Tenant want to enter into a new SLDT of the same land, the duration of the first let is added to the duration of the new let and the total period of let is more than 5 years

- if the Landlord and the Tenant of a 1991 Act tenancy agree under s2A of the 2003 Act to terminate the 1991 Act tenancy and substitute it with an MLDT

- if the Landlord and the Tenant of an LDT agree in writing to terminate the LDT prior to the termination date of that LD and enter into an MLDT of the same land

The final two examples involve conversion from pre-existing leases. The procedure to effect the conversion is found in s2A and s2B of the 2003 Act.

The Landlord and the Tenant must set out their agreement in writing and the agreement must narrate a termination date for the lease of not more than 30 days after the date of signing the agreement. The Landlord and the Tenant must then enter into an MLDT comprising the same land as was leased under the 1991 Act Tenancy or the LDT for at least as long as the existing lease had left to run, bearing in mind that the MLDT must be for a period of at least 10 years. In the period from the date of signing the agreement to the actual date of termination either party may revoke the agreement and the lease and revert to the status quo. The tenant is entitled to compensation for improvements on the termination of the 1991 Act tenancy or the LDT.

Where a Landlord enters into an MLDT with a Tenant who is a "new entrant" to farming the parties may, but are not obliged to, agree a break clause in the lease. Either the Landlord or the Tenant may trigger the operation of the break clause by giving notice to the other not more than two years but more than one year before the break date. The Tenant need give no reason to trigger the break clause but the Landlord must give reasons and may give such a notice only if the Tenant is either not farming in accordance with the rules of good husbandry or is otherwise failing to comply with a provision of the lease.

A "new entrant" is defined in The Agricultural Holdings (Modern Limited Duration Tenancies and Consequential etc. Provisions) (Scotland) Regulations 2017 as a person who has not, in the five years before entering into the MLDT, been a tenant under an LDT, MLDT, 1991 Act tenancy or an SLDT (for a period of 3 continuous years) and who has not in the five years before entering into the MLDT been a small landholder, a crofter or the owner of more than three hectares of agricultural land in aggregate. The regulations apply whether the tenant is an individual or has had control of a legal person such as a company, partnership or LLP which has been such a tenant or owner.

Repairing Tenancies

This is the final category of agricultural tenancy introduced by the 2016 Act. At the date of writing the provisions relating to Repairing

Tenancies are not yet fully in force.

The Repairing Tenancy will be a lease of agricultural land for a period of not less than 35 years which requires the Tenant to improve the land to bring it into a state capable of being farmed during the "repairing period" and during the remainder of the lease to farm in accordance with the rules of good husbandry.

The repairing period is a period to be agreed by the Landlord and the Tenant but cannot be for less than 5 years.

During that initial five-year period while the tenant is improving the land the Landlord will not be able to contend that the Tenant is not farming in accordance with the rules of good husbandry. The Landlord will be prevented from resuming land out of the tenancy during the repairing period and for a further 5 years after the repairing period has ended.

Most agricultural tenancies oblige the Landlord to provide, replace and renew fixed equipment on the holding or land rented.

The Repairing Tenancy is different.

S95 of the 2003 Act once enacted will provide that the parties to a Repairing Tenancy must agree a Schedule of fixed equipment within 90 days of the commencement of the tenancy. The Schedule will detail any fixed equipment which the Landlord does provide but there is no obligation on the Landlord to provide all the fixed equipment the Tenant needs for efficient production. It is the responsibility of the Tenant to provide the fixed equipment needed to maintain efficient production and thereafter to maintain, renew or replace that fixed equipment during the repairing period unless the lease provides to the contrary. At the end of the repairing period the Landlord will renew or replace the fixed equipment detailed in the Schedule unless the lease provides otherwise. The Tenant must maintain the fixed equipment specified in the Schedule in as good a condition as it was in at the expiry of the repairing period or when it was improved, provided, renewed or replaced.

There may be a break clause in the Repairing Tenancy but this cannot fall within the repairing period. At any time until the expiry of the repairing period the Tenant can give notice to terminate the Tenancy in writing more than one year but less than two years prior to the break date. As is the case for MLDTs to new entrants, the Tenant need give no reasons for exercising the break clause. The Landlord can only terminate the tenancy on the expiry of the repairing period. The Landlord must state reasons on the notice. The reason cannot be that the tenant is failing to farm in accordance with the rules of good husbandry and must relate to some other breach of the lease.

CHAPTER FOUR

GRAZING LEASES

Short term leases of less than one year for the purpose of grazing animals in grass fields are a feature of Scottish agriculture in practice. It is useful for both landlords and tenants to be able to enter into grazing leases without attracting security of tenure.

Provisions relating to such grazing leases were first introduced in the 1948 Act and repeated in the 1991 Act. They are now governed by s3 of the 2003 Act.

S3 2003 Act

The 2003 Act defines grazing leases as leases under which agricultural land is let for the purpose of it being used only for grazing or mowing during some specified period of the year which period must be no longer than 364 days.

There are therefore two conditions to be met – the use of the land must be for grazing or mowing for hay or silage and the lease must be for less than one year. The Landlord should therefore check the use being made of the land by the tenant during the course of the lease and that the tenant has removed all the stock at the date of termination.

The same land cannot be let to the same tenant on a grazing lease until at least one clear day has passed. It is possible to create in one document a series of grazing leases each for 364 days or less over a series of years.

Failed Grazing Leases

By their very definition grazing leases were short term arrangements. No grazing leases entered into under the 1991 Act legislation should still exist unless created as part of a series of grazing lets. Where a grazing lease entered into under the 1991 Act failed either because the tenant used the land for growing crops instead of grazing or the tenant did not physically vacate the land after 364 days a secure 1991 Act tenancy could result. Under the 2003 Act such a failed grazing let defaults to become a Short Limited Duration Tenancy.

Agistment

Agistment is another short-term arrangement which involves grazing animals. Agistment is not dealt with in the legislation. It exists as a contractual arrangement between the owner of the land and the owner of the animals. The contract is similar to a contract for services because the owner of the land provides some level of care for the animals. Typically a hill farmer will send some stock to be "over wintered" on a low land farm. Payment is usually made on a per head per week basis rather than as a rent.

CHAPTER FIVE

LEASES TO PARTNERSHIPS

History

As we have seen the creation of a 1991 Act tenancy has important consequences as it provides security of tenure not only for the tenant but potentially for following generations of the tenant's family. A 1991 Act tenancy can be perceived by Landlords as onerous and accordingly prior to the passing of the 2003 Act attempts were made in practice to circumvent the provisions of the 1991 Act.

A common method of avoiding security of tenure was the granting of a lease to a Limited Partnership in which the Landlord had some kind of interest. The Landlord or a member of the Landlord's family or other associate, such as a company in which the Landlord had an interest, would be the limited partner and the farmer (the true Tenant) would be the general partner. The Landlord would incur no liability for the partnership business but as a partner would be entitled to terminate the partnership.

The Landlord would then enter into a 1991 Act tenancy with the Limited Partnership as Tenant.

On or after the expiry of the stated duration of the 1991 Act tenancy, the Landlord as limited partner could serve notice to terminate the partnership. The Tenant no longer existed on the dissolution of the partnership. The provisions on tacit relocation is s3 of the 1991 Act could not apply and the lease came to an end.

2003 Act

S70 of the 2003 Act provides that if a 1991 Act tenancy is granted to a partnership in which the Landlord has an interest after the coming into force of the 2003 Act, then the partner or partners who are not the Landlord are treated as being the true tenant. So if Landlord A enters into a 1991 Act lease to ABC Farmers a limited partnership whose partners are A, B and C then B and C can exercise any rights pertaining to 1991 Act tenants. If the Landlord purports to terminate the tenancy by dissolving the partnership then B and C can give notice within 28 days of the purported termination that they intend to become joint tenants in their own right.

Leases to limited partnerships already in existence before the coming into force of the 2003 Act are dealt with in s72. The general partner can exercise any of the rights enjoyed by the tenants of 1991 Act tenancies and if the Landlord purports to terminate the tenancy by dissolving the partnership then the general partner can give notice within 28 days of the purported termination that he or she intends to become the tenant.

S73 then gives the Landlord a right to terminate the tenancy. A double notice procedure is required. The Landlord must give notice of his or her intention to terminate the tenancy more than two years but less than three years before the termination date of the tenancy or the expiry of the period of continuation if the tenancy is continuing on tacit relocation. The Landlord must thereafter serve a notice to quit more than one year but less than two years before the termination date. There must be a period of at least 90 days between the two notices.

When these proposals were first introduced to the Scottish Parliament as draft legislation some Landlords tried to terminate limited partnerships before the legislation came into force. A late amendment to the bill meant that Landlords who had acted in this way were prevented by s72 (10) as originally enacted from using the s73 double notice procedure.

A detailed discussion of the case of Salveson v Riddell 2013 SC (UKSC) 236 is beyond the scope of this book but the case dealt with a human rights challenge to power of the Scottish Government to exclude some Landlords from using the notice procedure in s73.

As a result of that case the Agricultural Holdings (Scotland) Act 2003 Remedial Order 2014 amended s72 and added s72A. S73 now applies to all tenancies created under s72(6) except "relevant tenancies" which are dealt with in the transitional provisions within the Order relating to ongoing cases.

CHAPTER SIX

FIXED EQUIPMENT

Definition

Fixed equipment is the expression used to describe equipment which belongs to the landlord but is provided to and used by the tenant for the purposes of farming the holding efficiently.

There is a statutory definition of fixed equipment in s 85(1) of the 1991 Act. Examples include walls, fences, gates, field drains, sheds, sheep fanks and importantly, the farm house and any farm cottages.

In terms of the legislation relating to both 1991 Act tenancies and the modern tenancies (SLDTs, LDTs and MLDTS) it is the responsibility of the Landlord to provide and eventually renew the fixed equipment. The tenant is only responsible for maintaining the fixed equipment in the condition it was provided in, fair wear and tear excepted. The relevant sections are s5 of the 1991 Act and s16 of the 2003 Act.

Obligations – 1991 Act Tenancies

The Landlord must put the fixed equipment in a thorough state of repair at the start of the tenancy and provide such fixed equipment as would allow a reasonably skilled farmer to maintain efficient production. The Landlord must also replace or renew any buildings or other fixed equipment as may be rendered necessary by fair wear and tear. The Tenant is thereafter responsible for maintaining the fixed equipment in that condition, fair wear and tear excepted. The obligation on the Landlord only extends to providing fixed equipment so that the Tenant can farm in the manner stipulated in the lease. Leases will often state that the farm is to be used as an arable farm or a stock farm or a mixed farm but specifically exclude use as a dairy farm. This is because the obligation on the Landlord to provide fixed equipment would be too onerous if provision of milking equipment was demanded by the Tenant.

These provisions do not apply to 1991 Act tenancies entered into before 1948 which are governed by the terms of the lease itself and the common law.

Obligations – SLDTs, LDTs and MLDTs

The Landlord must within 6 months of the commencement of the tenancy provide such fixed equipment as will enable the Tenant to maintain efficient production on the land as specified in the lease and put the fixed equipment so provided into the condition specified in the Schedule of Condition. Again, the Landlord is responsible for replacing or renewing buildings or other fixed equipment as may be rendered necessary by fair wear and tear during the course of the tenancy. The tenant is responsible for maintaining the fixed equipment in as good as state of repair as it was in when put into the condition specified in the Schedule of Condition or when it was improved, provided, renewed or replaced.

Obligations – Repairing Tenancies

The provisions of the 2016 Act which create Repairing Tenancies are not yet fully in force. S95 of the 2016 Act once enacted will provide that the parties to a Repairing Tenancy must agree a Schedule of fixed equipment within 90 days of the commencement of the tenancy. The Schedule will detail any fixed equipment which the Landlord does provide but there is no obligation on the Landlord to provide all the fixed equipment the Tenant needs for efficient production. It is the responsibility of the Tenant to provide the fixed equipment needed to maintain efficient production and thereafter to maintain, renew or replace that fixed equipment during the repairing period unless the lease provides to the contrary. At the end of the repairing period the Landlord will renew or replace the fixed equipment detailed in the Schedule unless the lease provides otherwise. The Tenant must maintain the fixed equipment specified in the Schedule in as good a condition as it was in at the expiry of the repairing period or when it was improved, provided, renewed or replaced.

Record of Condition/Schedule of Condition

S8 of the 1991 Act allows the landlord or tenant to request a record of the condition of the fixed equipment to be made at any time during the tenancy. Records are made at the joint expense of both parties and are usually made at the start of the tenancy. Records of Condition are not mandatory for 1991 Act tenancies. Schedules of Condition are mandatory for the modern tenancies. Records and Schedules are now usually photographic but many traditional 1991 Act tenancies are aged (or unwritten) and the record of condition might be vague if it exists at all. The Record of Condition is the starting point and ideally a tenant should be able to prove that he or she has adequately maintained the fixed equipment, by way of receipts for work carried out or confirmation that the tenant has done the work himself or herself.

S16 of the 2003 Act provides that the Landlord and the Tenant must agree a Schedule specifying the fixed equipment the Landlord will provide and the condition of that fixed equipment. The cost of preparing the Schedule is, unless otherwise agreed, to be split equally between the Landlord and the Tenant.

It is always a matter of proof whether the fixed equipment has reached the end of its natural life and requires to be replaced or whether the tenant is at fault for failing to maintain the fixed equipment so that its natural life was prolonged.

Farm Houses and Cottages

Where there is a farm house included in a tenancy these can often be quite antiquated and many Tenants make improvements themselves such as adding central heating. Farmhouses occupied by agricultural Tenants are at the moment exempt from meeting the Repairing Standard applicable to most residential let properties as defined in the Housing (Scotland) Act 2006 and need only reach the Tolerable Standard but legislation is being brought forward by the Scottish Government to bring farmhouses into the Repairing Standard category by 2027.

Post Lease Agreements

Prior to the passing of the 2003 Act, it was common practice for Landlords to contract out of the renewing or replacing obligation. The Landlord and the Tenant would enter into a "post lease agreement" which was a separate agreement sitting alongside the lease. These agreements typically provided that the Tenant would renew the fixed equipment themselves, relieving the Landlord of that responsibility.

S5(4D) of the 1991 Act as amended by the 2003 Act states that any agreement entered into after 27th November 2003 which purports to provide for the Tenant to bear any expense of any work which the Landlord is required to execute in order to fulfil his obligations under the lease shall be null and void.

Pre-2003 Act post lease agreements continue to have effect but the terms of s5 (4A) and (4B) of the 1991 Act apply. If there is an existing post lease agreement and the rent is reviewed, the Tenant can serve a notice to the effect that the post lease agreement is set aside. The Tenant can only serve such a notice if the fixed equipment is in reasonable repair or at least no worse than it was when the lease started. Landlords who initiate rent reviews where there is a post lease agreement should consider whether the benefit of the reviewed rent will outweigh the potential loss of the post lease agreement.

Remedies

A Landlord can serve notice demanding that a Tenant maintains specified Fixed Equipment and a Tenant can serve notice demanding that a Landlord provide or renew Fixed Equipment. The remedy for failure to comply with either notice is a referral to the Land Court.

CHAPTER SEVEN

WAYGOING AND TENANT'S IMPROVEMENTS

When an agricultural tenancy comes to an end both the Landlord and Tenant have certain statutory and contractual claims against each other. This chapter details the general rights a Tenant may have on waygoing, the specific right to claim the value of Tenant's improvements and the claims which can be made by a Landlord.

Waygoing – General

1991 Act Tenancies

The Tenant is entitled to remove all of the Tenant's own fixtures and buildings under s18 of the 1991 Act if certain conditions apply. The Tenant may not remove fixtures or buildings and claim compensation for improvements in relation to the same, the rent must be paid up to date, the fixtures or buildings must be removed within 6 months of the end of the tenancy and the Tenant must give the Landlord notice to allow the Landlord the opportunity to buy the fixtures or buildings at a fair value.

Where the Landlord serves a notice to quit (see Chapter 15) the tenant is entitled to receive a payment equivalent to one year's rent to compensate him or her for the upheaval of removing from the farm under s43 of the 1991 Act. This provision applies only to compensate the tenant when he or she is the innocent party against whom a notice to quit has been served. Where the Tenant has renounced the lease or the Landlord has terminated the lease by irritancy there is no claim under this section.

Where compensation for disturbance is payable the Tenant can also claim a re-organisation payment under s54. The payment is equivalent to four years' rent. S55 contains a number of exceptions referring back to the purpose for which the notice to quit was served under s22 and the Landlord suffering severe hardship.

The Land Reform (Scotland) Bill 2024 proposes that compensation for disturbance should also be available to a Tenant when a Landlord resumes land from the tenancy

Where the Tenant has been farming to a very high standard of efficiency ("high farming") and that will benefit any incoming Tenant then the outgoing Tenant is compensated under s44 by the amount of the value to the incoming Tenant.

SLDTs, LDTs and MLDTs

Where a Landlord resumes land from any of the modern types of tenancy, or as a result of that resumption the Tenant serves a notice to quit, the Tenant can claim compensation for disturbance and high farming under sections 52 and 53 of the 2003 Act. There is no provision for a claim for re-organisation payment.

Tenant's Improvements

The main claim a Tenant has at waygoing is a claim against the Landlord for the value of the Tenant's improvements.

There is a technical distinction between old improvements carried out before 1st November 1948 and new improvements carried out after that date. On the basis that there will be little residual value in improvements carried out before 1st November 1948, with the possible exception of drainage, this section concentrates on "new" improvements. These are covered by Schedule 5 of the 1991 Act.

The list of improvements is split into three sections:-

- Part 1 improvements where the Landlord's consent is needed
- Part 2 improvements where only notice to the Landlord is required and
- Part 3 improvements which do not require notice to or consent of the Landlord

The lists are quite technical but the most common types of improvement in practice are buildings, fences and drains all of which require notice to the landlord. Liming and fertilising fields are common improvements which do not require notice or consent. The current version of Schedule 5 was updated on 10th January 2019. The previous version of the Schedule should have been used in dealing with any Tenant's Amnesty documentation which is discussed in more detail below.

The Schedule stipulates a more formal process for more significant improvements because at the termination of the tenancy the Tenant is entitled to receive compensation for any improvements the Tenant has made and properly intimated. The level of the compensation is a payment equivalent to the value of the improvement to an incoming tenant. This method of calculation includes an element of depreciation because the value is assessed at the date of termination of the tenancy.

If the correct procedure has not been followed then the Landlord could potentially avoid liability for paying compensation to the

Tenant for the improvement.

The Land Reform (Scotland) Bill 2024 would introduce a whole new category of improvements which facilitate or enhance sustainable or regenerative agricultural production. These are listed in Part 4 of the Bill and include creating species-rich pasture, peatland restoration, conversion of the holding to an accredited standard of organic farming and the installation of buildings or structures for the creation or storage of renewable energy.

Tenants' Amnesty

The Scottish Government perceived that hardship could be caused to Tenants who had failed properly to intimate improvements. Chapter 8 of the 2016 Act introduced a three-year amnesty period ending on 13th June 2020 which allows Tenants to correct previous failures to follow the Schedule 5 procedure. The amnesty period was extended to 13th December 2020 by the Land Reform (Scotland) Act 2016 (Supplementary Provisions) (Coronavirus) Regulations 2020.

During that period of time it was open to the Landlord and the Tenant to agree a schedule of approved improvements.

No amnesty agreements can be entered into after 13th December 2020 so the detailed rules on the procedure for entering into such an agreement are no longer relevant.

Many amnesty agreements were completed by agreement between the Landlord and the Tenant and some were the subject of litigation in the Land Court.

It is important to establish when acting for a Tenant whether an amnesty agreement was entered into as it will be relevant when claiming compensation for improvements at the termination of the tenancy.

There was no immediate payment to the Tenant on signing an amnesty agreement. The amnesty agreement merely set out improvements which are accepted by the Landlord and for which compensation will be paid by the Landlord to the Tenant at the eventual waygoing.

Landlord's Claims at Waygoing

The Landlord's claims at waygoing are for dilapidations (s45), failure to maintain fixed equipment (s46) and compensation arising as a result of diversification and cropping of trees (s45A). This last provision compensates the Landlord:-

- if the size of the holding has been reduced by the diversification or

- provides a balancing payment calculated by setting off the loss of rent with the value of the trees and paid by or to the Landlord.

CHAPTER EIGHT

LANDLORD'S IMPROVEMENTS AND EMERGENCY IMPROVEMENTS

A Landlord who wishes to carry out a relevant improvement to an agricultural holding is required to give notice to the Tenant to that effect. A "relevant improvement" is defined in s14A of the 1991 Act as one which is not carried out at the request of the Tenant, in pursuance of an undertaking given by the Landlord to the Land Court or in pursuance of a direction given by the Scottish Ministers.

The notice must be dated and must state the names and designations of the Landlord and the Tenant, the address of the holding, the details of the improvement and the reasons why the Landlord considers the improvement is necessary to enable the Tenant to fulfil the Tenant's responsibilities to farm the holding in accordance with the rules of good husbandry.

Although most Tenants would welcome Landlord's improvements to their fixed equipment, the Tenant may object to such a notice if the objection is given to the Landlord in writing within 2 months of the date of the Landlord's notice. The Tenant's objection must be dated and state the Tenant's reasons why the improvement is not necessary to enable the Tenant to fulfil their responsibilities to farm the holding in accordance with the rules of good husbandry. A Landlord's improvement can result in an increase in rent and an increase in the Tenant's responsibility to maintain fixed equipment.

On receipt of such a notice of objection from the Tenant, the Landlord may apply to the Land Court for approval of the relevant improvement. The Land Court may approve the carrying out of the relevant improvement unconditionally or on such terms as appear to the Court to be appropriate.

Where the improvement is one carried out at the request of the Tenant, in pursuance of an undertaking given by the Landlord to the Land Court or in pursuance of a direction given by the Scottish Ministers, the Tenant has not objected to the Landlord's improvement notice or where the Land Court has approved the Landlord's improvement notice, the Landlord must give notice in writing to the Tenant stating the period during which the Landlord will carry out the improvement. Unless otherwise agreed between the Landlord and the Tenant, the work must not commence earlier than 2 weeks from the date of the notice. The period during which the Landlord's improvement will be carried out can be extended by notice given by the Landlord to the Tenant.

If a Landlord completes an improvement in these circumstances they can serve a notice on the Tenant within 6 months of completion of the improvement requiring an increase in the rent of the holding from the date of completion of the improvement by an amount equal to the increase in the rental value of the holding attributable to the carrying out of the improvement.

If a Landlord carries out an improvement without giving notice or if the Tenant objected to the notice and the Land Court has not approved the improvement, such an improvement is disregarded in any rent review, or in assessing the Tenant's responsibilities to farm in accordance with the rules of good husbandry and in relation to fixed equipment.

Similar provisions apply to the modern forms of tenancy, see ss10A to 10F of the 1991 Act.

Emergency Improvements

Either a Landlord or a Tenant can carry out an "emergency improvement" which means an improvement that is necessary for the purposes of:-

- protecting public health from infectious diseases, contamination or other hazards which constitute a danger to human health

- preventing a danger or a potential danger to public safety
- enabling the tenant to comply with the requirements of the Animal Health and Welfare Act 2006
- securing the provision of essential services including electricity and water supply services or
- remedying an accident or natural cause or force majeure which was exceptional and could not reasonably have been foreseen.

CHAPTER NINE

RENT REVIEW

This chapter considers how the rent payable in respect of any of the various kinds of agricultural tenancies is reviewed. S13 of the 1991 Act referred to "open market" rent reviews. There are so few 1991 Act tenancies left in Scotland that there was a scarcity of "comparable" evidence and there were arguments as to whether it was fair to use LDT or SLDT comparables where high rents had been achieved following advertising and competitive bidding. The amendments contained in the 2016 Act introducing Schedule 1A to the 1991 Act replaced the open market test with a "fair" rent test based on the productive capacity of the holding, the open market rent of any surplus residential accommodation and the open market rent of any land or fixed equipment on the holding used for a non-agricultural purpose.

Notice

S13 of the 1991 Act simply provided that either the Landlord or the Tenant of an agricultural holding may, following notice in writing served on the other party, have determined by the Land Court the rent properly payable in respect of the holding.

The provisions of Schedule 1A provide much more detail as to what information should be contained within the rent notice. The rent review notice must be dated and state the names and designations of the Landlord and the Tenant of the holding, the name and address of the holding, the rent currently payable, the rent the person serving the notice proposes should be payable and the date by which the landlord and the tenant must reach agreement on what the rent payable should be. Either the landlord or the tenant can serve a rent review notice.

The rent review notice must be accompanied by information in writing explaining the basis on which the rent proposed by the person serving the notice has been calculated.

Timing

A rent notice must be served more than one year but less than two years before the date from which the new rent is intended to take effect. Under s13 the timing of the rent notice was tied to the date when the lease could in theory have been terminated, usually 28th November. This led to a flurry of rent review notices being served in November each year.

Under Schedule 1A the parties can serve notice at any time by fixing a rent agreement date not more than two years but not less than one year from the date of the rent review notice. If the landlord wishes to review the rent with effect from 1st June 2020 he or she would require to serve a rent review notice no later than 31st May 2019 and no earlier than 1st June 2018.

The rent payable in respect of an agricultural holding can only be reviewed every three years. A review can therefore only take place three years after the start of the tenancy or the date when the rent was last reviewed.

A review for this purpose includes a determination by the Land Court that the rent should remain unchanged.

Sometimes the rent changes without a review, for example if the landlord resumes land and reduces the rent, if the landlord opts to tax the land and charges VAT on the rent or if the VAT rate changes. These changes in the amount of rent payable are not reviews of the rent and do not affect the three-year rule.

Referral to the Land Court

Following service of the rent review notice the parties negotiate and seek to agree a fair rent for the holding.

If the parties reach agreement as to what rent should be payable that agreement constitutes a review for the purposes of the three-year rule.

If they cannot agree then either party, not just the party who served the notice, can refer the question of what the rent payable in respect of the holding should be to the Land Court.

If there is no referral the rent notice falls and the rent is not considered to have been reviewed for the three-year rule and accordingly either party could raise a fresh rent review notice.

The Land Court can vary the rent or determine that the rent should remain unchanged. If the Land Court determines that the rent should remain unchanged that determination counts as a review of the rent for the purposes of the three-year rule so neither party can serve a rent notice for three years after the date of determination.

Open Market Rent

The concept of an "open market" rent review is familiar to commercial law practitioners. The rent fixed by the Land Court was in terms of s13 (3) of the 1991 Act to be such as the holding might reasonably be expected to achieve when let on the open market by a willing Landlord to a willing Tenant.

The Land Court was directed to consider:-

- evidence of comparable rents and
- the current economic conditions in the relevant sector of agriculture

The Land Court was directed to disregard:-

- the fact that there is a tenant in occupation of the holding
- any distortion in rent due to scarcity of lets
- any Tenant's improvements
- any Landlord's improvements which had been financed by government grant
- the continuous adoption by the Tenant of a higher standard of farming or a system of farming more beneficial to the holding than was required by the lease or normally practised in the area
- any dilapidations or damage to the fixed equipment caused by the Tenant
- any reduction in the rental value resulting from conservation activities or the use of the land for non-agricultural purposes

Fair Rent

The replacement for the "open market" test is a new reference in Schedule 1A of the 1991 Act to a "fair rent".

In determining what a fair rent for the holding would be the Land Court is directed to consider the productive capacity of the holding, the open market rent of any surplus residential accommodation and the open market rent of any land or fixed equipment used for a non-agricultural purpose.

The Scottish Government may make regulations about how the productive capacity of the holding is to be determined. In the Scottish Government Report "Testing the Rent Review System" (published 26th January 2018) the productive capacity of a holding was defined as meaning the sustainable yield of agricultural products that would reasonably be expected from the holding under a system of farming suitable to it when farmed by a competent, efficient and experienced farmer with adequate resources for that system.

The Land Court must also have regard to the open market rent of any surplus accommodation so if the holding includes a cottage no longer required for a farm worker which the Tenant is renting out that will be taken into account.

A Landlord can in some circumstances resume residential property on the holding which is no longer required to accommodate farm workers, see Chapter 10.

Finally the Land Court is directed to have regard to the open market value of any fixed equipment or land which is not being used for agricultural purposes so if the Tenant farmer has set up a farm shop in one of the sheds on the agricultural holding, the rental value of that shop will be assessed on an open market commercial basis.

The "open market" rent to be assessed for any surplus residential accommodation or diversified activity is defined as being the rent which might reasonably be expected if the property in question were let on the open market by a willing landlord to a willing tenant.

If the new rent payable in respect of the holding is determined by the Land Court to be 30% or more higher or 30% or more lower than the rent currently payable either the Landlord or the Tenant can apply to have the new rent phased in. Where the Land Court receives such an application and considers that either the Landlord or the Tenant would suffer "undue hardship" if the rent was made payable from the rent agreement date then the court can make an order to phase in the new rent over a period of three years.

The rent payable for the year after the rent agreement date would be the original rent plus one third of the difference between the original rent and the new rent and for the following year the original rent plus two thirds of the difference between the original rent and the new rent. In the third year the new rent would be paid in full.

The proposals on rent review in the Land Reform (Scotland) Bill 2024 would remove the specific reference to subletting surplus residential accommodation although such subletting could still fall within the category of use of fixed equipment for a non-agricultural purpose.

The 2024 Bill proposes to add two further considerations being the rent payable on similar holdings and the prevailing economic conditions in the sectors of agriculture relevant to the holding. These amendments would mean a return to consideration of comparable evidence of rents paid for similar holdings and a move back towards an open market rent test.

SLDTs, LDTs, MLDTs and Repairing Tenancies

There are no statutory provisions on review of rent payable in respect of SLDTs due to their short duration. The lease may contain rent review provisions which would be particularly relevant if the lease lasts for 5 years. If the tenancy converts to an MLDT then the statutory provisions would apply.

The terms of the lease itself also govern the review of rents in LDTs and MLDTs. However s9 (A1) of the 2003 Act as amended by the 2016 Act provides that upwards only rent review clauses or provisions whereby rent reviews may be initiated only by Landlords are void and the rent under a lease containing such a provision is instead reviewed and determined in accordance with s9.

The rent payable under a Repairing Tenancy is always to be reviewed and determined in accordance with s9.

S9A details the information to be included in the rent review notice and s9B applies a "fair rent" test. The provisions in both of those sections are broadly similar to the provisions of Schedule 1A.

CHAPTER TEN

RESUMPTION

This chapter deals with the circumstances in which Landlords may resume land let as part of an Agricultural Holding and the consequences of such resumption.

1991 Act Tenancies

S29 of the 1991 Act allows Landlords to resume land in a number of limited circumstances being:- the erection of farm workers' houses, the provision of gardens for farm workers house, construction of roads, planting trees, extracting minerals, creating allotments or small holdings and creating water courses or reservoirs.

Most written leases contain a resumption clause allowing Landlords to resume for wider non-agricultural purposes, most commonly house building. Such resumption clauses are commonly drafted to allow Landlords to resume for any purpose other than agriculture. The resumption clause will often stipulate the notice the Landlord requires to give to the tenant and any particular provisions on compensation.

If the lease allows the Landlord to resume land from the holding for agriculture purposes any resumption notice served is subject to the provisions of s22 of the 1991 Act, ie a counter notice can be served by the Tenant and the resumption notice is of no effect unless the Landlord applies to the Land Court and the Land Court upholds the notice.

Where a written lease does not contain a resumption clause the Landlord has no right to resume land let as part of the agricultural holding other than in terms of s29. Where there is an unwritten lease there can be no right to resume other than in terms of s29.

Even where resumption is permitted in terms of the lease for non-agricultural purposes a tenant may still challenge a resumption notice by application to the Land Court on the basis that the purpose for the resumption stated in the notice does not in fact exist or that the resumption would be a fraud on the lease.

Fraud on the Lease

A resumption notice is a fraud on the lease, or contrary to the good faith of the lease, if the resumption would prevent the tenant from continuing to farm the holding as an agricultural holding. A resumption of a small area of ground from an already small agricultural holding could be more likely to be a fraud on the lease than the resumption of a larger area of ground from a larger agricultural holding.

Compensation

Whilst the resumption clause in the lease may determine the specific amount of compensation to which a Tenant is entitled, or possibly state that no compensation is payable, a Tenant is always entitled, as an alternative to following the terms of the lease, to claim the statutory rights to which he or she would have been entitled had the resumption proceeded under s29. Those rights are:-

- To have the rent for the holding reduced
- To compensation for disturbance, being the equivalent of one year's rent of the area resumed

- To an additional payment for re-organisation, being the equivalent of four year's rent of the area resumed

2003 Act Tenancies

S17 of the 2003 Act sets out the terms on which a Landlord may resume land let under an SLDT, an LDT or a MLDT.

The Landlord may resume land for any non-agricultural purpose for which planning permission would be required if that planning permission has in fact been obtained.

Notice of Resumption must be given in writing, must stipulate the date of the resumption and must be served on the Tenant at least one year before that date.

The Tenant can respond by giving a counter notice to the Landlord within 28 days of receipt of the Notice of Resumption terminating the tenancy as a whole. The termination will take effect from the date of the proposed resumption as stipulated in the Notice of Resumption.

If the lease continues the Tenant is entitled to a reduction in rent proportionate to the area resumed from the holding and also payment of an amount in respect of depreciation in value of the remaining holding. In determining the amount of the proportionate reduction, account is to be taken of any benefit or relief allowed to the Tenant under the lease of the area resumed.

When s96 of the 2016 Act comes into force the Landlord in a Repairing Tenancy is prohibited from resuming land from the tenancy during the repairing period and for a period of five years after the expiry of the repairing period.

Land Reform (Scotland) Bill 2024

The Land Reform (Scotland) Bill 2024 proposes some changes to the procedure on resumption. If enacted the proposals state that a resumption notice must be served not less than a year before the proposed date of resumption which date must be given in the notice. The Landlord will also be obliged to send a copy of the notice of resumption to the Tenant Farming Commissioner.

The Bill provides for compensation to be paid by the Landlord to the Tenant with provisions for assessment of level of that compensation. The compensation payment is to reflect a one-half share of the difference between the open market value of the land resumed and the value subject to the tenancy.

CHAPTER ELEVEN

DIVERSIFICATION

In order to attract the statutory protections outlined in the preceding chapters an agricultural holding must be used for "agriculture" as defined in s85 of the 1991 Act, i.e. for horticulture, fruit growing, seed growing, dairy farming, livestock breeding and keeping, the use of land as grazing land, meadow land, osier land, market gardens and nursery grounds, and the use of land for woodlands where that use is ancillary to the farming of land for other agricultural purposes.

However, since 2003 tenant farmers have had a right to "diversify" or use their tenanted land for non-agricultural purposes.

Common examples of farm diversifications are farm shops, holiday accommodation and wind or hydro energy schemes all of which can provide additional income to supplement the farming business.

2003 Act

Part 3 of the 2003 Act applies to tenants of 1991 Act Tenancies, Limited Duration Tenancies, Modern Limited Duration Tenancies and Repairing Tenancies. Short Limited Duration Tenancies are not covered by this part of the Act and accordingly tenants of Short Limited Duration Tenancies are not entitled to diversify.

Tenancies covered by Part 3 do not terminate simply because the land or part of it is being used for a non-agricultural purpose and any provision in a lease which prohibits use for a non-agricultural purpose is of no effect. The provisions do not have retrospective effect. Any diversifications existing before the introduction of the protections of the 2003 Act continue to be a breach of the terms of the lease where non-agricultural use is prohibited in terms of the lease or the Landlord has not consented to the diversified use.

Sub-letting

Where a lease prohibits sub-letting and that prohibition stops the Tenant from diversifying then the tenant is entitled to sub-let in contravention of the lease provided the sub-letting is ancillary to the tenant's diversification, e.g. a holiday let or lease for a renewable energy project.

Notice of Diversification

In order for these provisions to apply the tenant must serve notice on the Landlord (known as a "notice of diversification") in writing not less than 70 days before the date on which the diversification is due to commence.

The notice of diversification must specify what the diversification is, what land will be affected, any changes to the land the Tenant proposes to make and the date when the Tenant proposes the diversification should start.

If changes to the land are proposed or the diversification will be in furtherance of a business the Tenant must also detail in the notice of diversification how the work will be financed and managed.

Landlord's Response

On receiving a notice of diversification the Landlord can object, request more information or accept but impose conditions.

The Landlord may on one occasion only and within 30 days of the giving of the notice of diversification request further relevant information relating to the intended use of the land or management or financing of the business. If the Landlord requests further information the Tenant must provide that further information within 30 days.

If the Landlord wishes to object this must be done within 60 days of receipt of the notice of diversification or the additional information, if requested.

The grounds on which the Landlord can object to the notice of diversification are that the intended use would lessen significantly the amenity of the land itself or the surrounding area, substantially prejudice the use of the land for agricultural purposes in the future, be detrimental to the sound management of the estate of which the land forms part or cause the Landlord to suffer severe hardship.

Referral to the Land Court

It is no longer enough for the Landlord to object to the notice of diversification, the Landlord must follow up that objection with a referral to the Land Court within 60 days of the notice of objection. This change was introduced by s121 of the Land Reform (Scotland) Act 2016. Under the previous law where the Landlord objected it was for the Tenant to refer to the Land Court for a decision on whether the Landlord's objection was reasonable. If no referral to the Land Court is made by the Landlord then the objection ceases to have effect. The Land Court can uphold the objection in which case the diversification does not proceed or determine that the objection is unreasonable in which case the diversification can take effect either from the originally appointed date or such other date as the Land Court might intimate.

The Land Court also has jurisdiction to determine whether any conditions imposed by the Landlord are unreasonable. The Land Court can remove any unreasonable condition and impose on the tenant any such reasonable conditions as the Court considers to be appropriate.

The Landlord may withdraw the objection within 60 days of the same having been notified. The withdrawal must be intimated to the Tenant in writing and can be subject to specified conditions applying to the diversification.

Timber

S42 of the 2003 Act covers the Tenant's right to harvest timber. Where trees are planted by the Tenant after 27th November 2003 and the Tenant harvests the timber from those trees then the timber belongs to the Tenant. If the lease or any other agreement in writing contains a provision whereby any such timber belongs to the Landlord then that provision is of no effect unless there is specific provision for a reduction in rent or other financial compensation to the tenant as a result of that provision.

Rent Review

Schedule 1A of the 1991 Act governs rent review and provides that when a rent is reviewed the Land Court in determining a "fair rent" for the holding should have regard to the open market rent of any fixed equipment provided by the Landlord or land forming part of the holding which is used for a non-agricultural purpose. This means that the Tenant may well have to pay an open market commercial rent for that part of the leased subjects which is used for a diversified purpose such as a farm shop, holiday accommodation or a renewable energy development.

Compensation

S45A of the 1991 Act governs compensation payable by or due to Landlords and Tenants as a result of a Tenant's diversification.

A Landlord is entitled to recover compensation from a Tenant at the end of a tenancy if the Landlord can show that the value of the holding has been reduced because of the diversified use. The compensation is based on the reduction in the value of the holding.

Likewise, a Tenant is entitled to recover compensation from a Landlord at the end of a tenancy if the Tenant can show that the value of the holding has been increased because of the diversified use. The compensation is based on the value to an incoming tenant of the diversified use. No compensation is payable to a Tenant where the diversification means the land or fixed equipment is rendered unsuitable for agricultural use by an incoming tenant.

Land Reform (Scotland) Bill 2024

Under s15 of the Bill a Tenant will be entitled to include in any diversification notice information confirming any environmental benefit that is intended to be provided in using the land for the diversified purpose.

Where the Land Court is considering whether or not to uphold a Landlord's objection to a diversification notice they must in terms of s17 of the Bill take into account whether use of land for the non-agricultural purpose is likely to have a positive effect in facilitating or enhancing sustainable or regenerative agricultural production on the whole of the land comprised in the lease, or on the environment generally, and consider whether such positive effects are likely and whether they outweigh any negative effects.

As stated above, compensation can be payable to a Tenant at the end of a tenancy because of the Tenant's diversification but this can be reduced if the land has been rendered unsuitable for use for agriculture by an incoming tenant. The 2024 Bill would replace that test with "use of the whole of the land comprised in the holding for the purposes of sustainable and regenerative agriculture by an incoming tenant has been substantially prejudiced".

CHAPTER TWELVE

RIGHT TO BUY

Part 2 of the 2003 Act gave Tenants of 1991 Act tenancies a limited right to buy the land comprised within the tenancy. This right does not extend to tenants of SLDTs, LDTs, MLDTs or Repairing Tenancies.

The 1991 Act Tenant's right to buy remains passive and is only activated where the Landlord proposes to sell the land. The spectre of a more pro-active or absolute right to buy applying to all agricultural tenancies, even where the Landlord had no intention of selling, has haunted attempts by legislators to make more land available to rent and is anecdotally one of the biggest disincentives to Landlords considering renting out land.

Registration – 2003 Act

The Tenant registers their right to buy by completing and submitting Form RCIL (AT) Notice of Interest in Acquiring Land and submitting the form to the Keeper of the Registers of Scotland. The form requires to be completed with details of the Tenant, the Landlord and the land comprised within the tenancy. A plan should be docquetted and lodged along with the application. The Keeper charges a fee, currently £40 for a first registration and £25 for a renewal.

A copy of the application form should be sent by recorded delivery to the Landlord. On receipt of the notice the Keeper must register the interest and send an extract of the registration to the Tenant.

The Landlord may, by notice in writing addressed to the Keeper, challenge the registration of the Tenant's interest in acquiring land on the grounds that any matter in the extract is inaccurate. The Keeper must make enquiries following receipt of such a challenge and must rescind the Tenant's interest if the inaccuracy is material and may amend the registration if the inaccuracy is not material. In practice the Keeper does not engage in disputes as to whether inaccuracies are material or not and simply publishes any correspondence between the Keeper, the Landlord or the Tenant alongside the registration.

Transfer of Land

Where a Landlord proposes to transfer the land over which a Tenant's right to buy has been registered the Landlord must give notice of the proposed transfer to the Tenant and copy that notice to the Keeper. The notice must be given in the form set out in Schedule 2 of the Agricultural Holdings (Forms) (Scotland) Regulations 2004.

S27 of the 2003 Act specifies various types of transfer which do not trigger the tenant's right to buy and which do not require the landlord to serve notice. These include:-

- gifts
- transfers in implement of a court order or under compulsory acquisition
- transfers between spouses
- transfers in implement of missives or option agreements in existence before the registration of the right to buy and
- transfers to statutory undertakers.

S27(2) contains anti-avoidance provisions whereby if an individual transfer forms part of a scheme to avoid the requirements of Part 2 of the 2003 Act then the transfer is deemed to be a transfer for which notice to the tenant should be given.

Giving Notice or Taking Action

Where the Landlord gives notice to the Tenant of the Landlord's intention to sell the land, or where the Landlord should have given notice but did not and then "takes any action" with a view to the transfer of the land, the Tenant's right to buy the land is triggered.

Taking any action with a view to the transfer of the land is defined as:-

- advertising the land for sale or
- entering into negotiations with another person or proceeding further with any transfer of land which was initiated prior to the notice of interest being registered (but not if the transfer is in implement of missives or an option agreement already concluded before the right to buy is registered).

Purchase

Where notice of the Landlord's intention to sell has been served on the Tenant, the Tenant then gives notice under s29 within 28 days of receipt of the Landlord's notice and proceeds to buy the land in accordance with s32.

Where notice of the landlord's intention to sell should have been given but was not in fact given then the tenant can serve notice on the third party who acquired from the landlord in contravention of the tenant's right to buy. That notice must be served within three years of the transfer to the third party.

Copies of all notices served under s29 must be sent to the Keeper of the Register. If the Tenant does not serve notice within either 28 days or 3 years or the Tenant serves notice under s29 (5) that he or she does not intend to proceed with the purchase the right to buy is extinguished. The Tenant cannot re-register a notice of interest in acquiring the same land within 12 months of the date when the first right to buy expired or within 12 months if the land has been transferred to a third party who is required to serve notice, for example a third party to whom the land had been gifted subject to the notice of acquisition.

Offer

S32 governs the procedure for exercise of the Tenant's right to buy. It is for the Tenant to make an offer at a price agreed between the Landlord and the Tenant and failing agreement as assessed by a valuer appointed under s33.

The date of entry and the date of payment of the price must be not later than 6 months from the date when the Tenant gave notice of the Tenant's intention to buy or where the valuer's assessment has been appealed no later than 2 months after the appeal has been determined or abandoned or such later date as the Landlord and the Tenant may agree.

If the Tenant has not concluded missives or taken all reasonable steps towards concluding missives within the timescales set out in s32 the Landlord may apply to the Land Court for an order directing that the Tenant conclude missives and to incorporate in those missives any conditions the Land Court may specify. If the Tenant does not comply with the Land Court's order the right to buy is extinguished. Even where the Landlord has not applied to the Land Court for a formal order the right to buy is extinguished by s32 (8) where the Tenant has not "within a reasonable period", having regard to the timescales set out in s32(3), concluded missives with the seller.

Valuation

The valuer is appointed by agreement between the Landlord and Tenant and failing agreement by the Land Court. If the land is situated on an estate where more than one Tenant is exercising their right to buy the valuer is to be appointed by agreement between the Landlord and at least half of the Tenants exercising their right to buy. The cost of the valuation is borne by the Tenant or if there are a number of Tenants on the same estate all exercising their right to buy, equally between those tenants.

S34 sets out the matters the valuer should take into account and also those matters which should be disregarded. The valuer is directed to assess the value of the land on a willing seller/willing buyer basis but taking into account:-

- the fact that the buyer is a "sitting Tenant"

- whether there exists a third party who would pay above market value for the land because of some particular characteristic which relates peculiarly to that person's interest in buying it

- when the selling Landlord would, in the natural course of events, have been likely to recover vacant possession

- the terms of any sporting lease affecting the land

- any moveable items included in the sale

And disregarding:-

- any unlawful use of the land
- any marketing period if the land were sold on the open market
- any tenant's improvements
- any fixed equipment belonging to the Tenant
- any increase or decrease in value because of the use of the land for a diversified or conservation purpose
- any dilapidations

The valuer is also directed in s34 (4) to consider the value of the estate as a whole both with and without the land being valued. The price eventually assessed by the valuer as payable by the tenant is to be the higher of the valuation of the land itself or the valuation resulting from comparing the difference between the estate being sold on the open market including and excluding the land itself. The Tenant could end up paying a higher price for the land if the price representing the loss to the Landlord is greater than the valuation.

The valuer must invite representations from the Landlord and the Tenant and have regard to those representations. The valuer must produce a notice in writing specifying the price to be paid by the Tenant and the valuer's methodology within 6 weeks of being appointed.

Appeal

Either the Landlord or the Tenant may appeal the valuer's decision within 21 days of receipt of the same. The appeal lies to the Lands Tribunal not the Land Court although the Lands Tribunal may under s38 refer back to the Land Court any issues of law which arise in terms of the 1991 Act.

The Lands Tribunal may reassess the value of the land or, where appropriate, the estate as a whole and determine the price. The decision of the Lands Tribunal is final and there is no further appeal.

Part 2 of the 2003 Act applies to owners of land but also to holders of heritable securities who have a right to sell as enforcing heritable creditors.

Registration – 2016 Act

S99 (2) of the Land Reform (Scotland) Act 2016 was intended to remove the requirement for registration of the Tenant's right to buy. The 2003 Act was intended to be amended by the 2016 Act to the effect that where the Landlord of a 1991 Act tenancy or a heritable creditor enforcing a standard security over land comprised in a 1991 Act tenancy proposes to transfer the land to another person notice must be given to the Tenant. The excluded transactions detailed in s27 and discussed above would continue to apply with the exception of the exclusion where missives or an option were concluded prior to registration as there is no longer any requirement to register.

S99 has not been brought into force.

Registration – 2024 Bill

The Land Reform (Scotland) Bill 2024 will empower the Scottish Ministers to make further provision for or in connection with the registration by Tenants of 1991 Act tenancies of their interests in acquiring the land comprised in their leases. It appears therefore that the idea of a Tenant's right to buy which exists in the general law without some kind of formal registration has been dropped. It remains to be seen what level of formality the Scottish Ministers will require when the new provisions are introduced.

General Partners

The Tenant's right to buy applies only to Tenants with 1991 Act tenancies but does include the general partner of a limited partnership where the limited partnership is the Tenant. This means that the general partner can register their right to buy the land tenanted by the limited partnership even although the limited partner is the Landlord or a corporate body controlled by the Landlord. S35 provides that where the general partner is buying the land and a valuer has been appointed the valuer should disregard the fact of the tenancy so the general partner (unlike a normal 1991 Act tenant) does not benefit from any reduction in value because there is a sitting Tenant.

2016 Act – Order for Sale

S100 of the 2016 Act applies where the Land Court has made an order or an arbiter has made an award requiring a Landlord to remedy a material breach of the Landlord's obligations to the Tenant and where that Landlord has failed to comply with such an order or award to a material extent. In such circumstances the Tenant may apply to the Land Court for an "order for sale" which is an order that the Tenant has the right to buy the land comprised in the lease. The Land Court will only make such an order if satisfied that the Landlord has failed to comply with the order or award in a material regard, that failure substantially and adversely affects the Tenant's ability to fulfil the Tenant's responsibilities to farm the holding in accordance with the rules of good husbandry, greater hardship would be caused by not making the order than by making it and in all the circumstances it is appropriate. Detailed procedure for buying and valuation are set out in Chapter 4 of the 2016 Act, amending s38 of the 2003 Act.

CHAPTER THIRTEEN

ASSIGNATION, SUBLETTING AND RELINQUISHMENT

This chapter covers transfer of a Tenant's interest in an agricultural lease by assignation or sub-letting and also considers the new provisions on relinquishment contained in the 2016 Act.

Assignation – 1991 Act Tenancies

Assignation of 1991 Act tenancies was always possible but only if expressly permitted by the terms of the lease.

The 2003 Act added s10A to the 1991 Act and for the first time gave agricultural Tenants a limited right to assign their tenancy even if prohibited from doing so by the terms of the lease. Initially the assignee could only be a "near relative" of the Tenant, that is any person entitled under the Succession (Scotland) Act 1964 to succeed to the estate of the Tenant.

The 2016 Act further extended this category which now includes spouses or civil partners of near relatives, nephews and nieces, brothers-in-law and sisters-in-law, step-children and spouses or civil partners and descendants of step-children.

Notice

The Tenant must give the Landlord notice in writing of the intention to assign the lease. The notice must include particulars of the proposed assignee, the terms on which the proposed assignation is made and the date on which it is to take effect.

Withholding Consent

The Landlord can withhold consent to the assignation if there are reasonable grounds for doing so. Two examples of grounds for withholding consent are given. These are that the proposed assignee has insufficient financial resources to pay the rent or maintain the holding or does not have sufficient training or experience to farm with reasonable efficiency.

If the person to whom the lease is assigned is a near relative the grounds for withholding consent are more limited. The Landlord can only withhold consent to the assignation to a near relative if the person is not of good character, has insufficient resources to pay the rent or maintain the holding or does not have sufficient training or experience to farm with reasonable efficiency. The Landlord cannot rely on any other "reasonable grounds" in the case of a near relative.

The ground specifying lack of training or experience does not apply if the proposed assignee is engaged in or will begin within 6 months of the date of the notice relevant training in agriculture which the proposed assignee is expected satisfactorily to complete within 4 years and has made arrangements for the holding to farmed efficiently in the interim.

The Landlord has 30 days from the date of receipt of the notice to intimate that he or she withholds consent. If the Landlord does not respond then consent is implied and the assignation goes ahead.

Land Court

If the Landlord does withhold consent then the lease continues with the existing Tenant. The Tenant may apply to the Land Court for a finding that the Landlord's grounds for withholding consent are not reasonable or not within the limited grounds for withholding consent to an assignation to a near relative.

If the Landlord has not withheld consent and the assignation is to proceed the Tenant must then complete the process by signing a formal assignation in favour of the assignee and intimating the fact that the assignation has now taken place to the Landlord.

Assignation – 2003 Act Tenancies

The tenant's interest in LDTs and MLDTs can be assigned in terms of s7 and s7B of the 2003 Act following similar procedures to those outlined above for 1991 Act tenancies.

SLDTs may not be assigned.

When Repairing Tenancies become law, s106 of the 2016 Act will provide that these tenancies may be assigned by the Tenant during the repairing period but only with the consent of the Landlord. The Landlord may withhold consent on any reasonable grounds including concerns that the proposed assignee may not be able to pay the rent or may lack the necessary skills and expertise to manage and improve the land to bring it back into a state capable of being farmed.

Subletting

Subletting of 1991 Act tenancies is only permitted where expressly provided by the lease and most 1991 Act leases prohibit subletting. If the lease is unwritten there is no implied right to sublet.

Tenants of land let under LDTs and MLDTs can only sublet where expressly provided by the lease. Tenants of land let under SLDTs are expressly prohibited from sub-letting by s6 of the 2003 Act.

When the provisions relating to Repairing Tenancies are fully brought into force subletting during the repairing period will be expressly prohibited by s7C of the 2003 ACT. Thereafter subletting is permitted only if the lease expressly so provides.

Relinquishment

It has always been possible for Tenants to negotiate a waygoing with their Landlords. If a Tenant wishes to retire from farming the negotiation usually involves a payment from the Landlord to the Tenant in recognition that the Landlord is recovering vacant possession of the holding which may otherwise be assigned or bequeathed by the Tenant. If the Landlord did not wish to enter into such negotiations voluntarily the Tenant could not compel him or her to do so. s32A of the 1991 Act as introduced by the Land Reform (Scotland) Act 2016 allows Tenants of 1991 Act tenancies to serve a Notice of Intention to Relinquish the holding on the Landlord. The notice must be in writing, dated and must state the names and designations of the Landlord and the Tenant, the name and address of the holding, the rent currently payable, when the rent was last reviewed and any improvements carried out by the tenant. The Notice must also indicate that the Tenant will quit the holding provided the Landlord pays compensation as calculated by a formula in s32L.

A copy of the Notice of Intention to Relinquish must be served on the Tenant Farming Commissioner.

If the Landlord does not pay the compensation assessed using the formula then the Tenant can assign the tenancy for value on the open market to a person who is either a "new entrant to farming" or who is "progressing in farming".

A "new entrant" is defined in The Agricultural Holdings (Modern Limited Duration Tenancies and Consequential etc. Provisions) (Scotland) Regulations 2017 as a person who has not, within the previous five years, been a tenant under an LDT, MLDT, 1991 Act tenancy or an SLDT (for a period of 3 continuous years) and who has not in the previous five years been a small landholder, a crofter or the owner of more than three hectares of agricultural land in aggregate. The regulations apply whether the tenant is an individual or has had control of a legal person such as a company, partnership or LLP which has been such a tenant or owner.

A person "Progressing in farming" is defined in the Agricultural Holdings (Relinquishment and Assignation) (Scotland) Regulations 2020 as a person who does not hold two or more "relevant interests" or will not become by virtue of the assignation a person who holds two or more "relevant interests".

A person has a "relevant interest" where that person (or any legal entity of which that person has control) is:-

- the Tenant of more than 3 hectares comprised in a Short Limited Duration Tenancy, a Limited Duration Tenancy, a Modern Limted Duration Tenancy or a 1991 Act Lease.

- a crofter

- a small landholder
- the owner of more than 3 hectares of agricultural land on a single title.

The Tenant may not serve a Notice of Intention to Relinquish if any of the following conditions apply:-

- The Tenant has already served a notice to quit on the Landlord.
- The Tenant has failed to comply with a written demand by the Landlord to pay rent or remedy a breach of a condition of the tenancy which breach is capable of being remedied and is not inconsistent with the Tenant's responsibilities to farm according to the rules of good husbandry.
- The Landlord has served an incontestable Notice to Quit.
- The Landlord has served a contestable Notice to Quit and still has time to apply to the Land Court for consent to the operation of the Notice to Quit or has applied to the Land Court which has yet to reach a decision or the Land Court has consented to the application and either no appeal has been made, the time limit for appeal has not expired or the Land Court's decision has been upheld on appeal.
- The Landlord has served a contestable Notice to Quit and the Land Court has refused consent to the operation of the same but the time limit for appeal has not expired, an appeal has been made but not determined or the decision of the Land Court to refuse consent has been quashed on appeal.

Valuation

On receipt of a copy Notice of Intention to Relinquish the Tenant Farming Commissioner must within 14 days appoint a valuer to carry out the assessment of the value of the land and the improvements carried out by the Landlord and the Tenant and thereafter calculate the amount payable by the Landlord to the Tenant. The Tenant Farming Commissioner must give notice in writing to the Landlord and the Tenant of the name and address of the valuer. The Landlord and Tenant have 14 days from receipt of the notice to apply to the Land Court to object to the appointed valuer.

The Tenant is responsible for paying the valuer's expenses.

The formula in s32L directs the valuer to calculate the open market value of the holding and then deduct from that amount the current value of the holding subject to the tenancy. That net amount is then split equally between the Landlord and the Tenant (amount A). The valuer then calculates the value of the Tenant's improvements and deducts the value of the Landlord's improvements (amount B). The valuer then adds amount A to amount B to give the total payable by the Landlord to the Tenant.

The payment to the Tenant is therefore the value of the Tenant's improvements plus a one-half share of the uplift in the value of the holding with vacant possession over the value of the holding subject to a 1991 Act tenancy.

The valuer has 8 weeks from the last date on which either the Landlord or the Tenant could have objected to his or her appointment within which to serve a Notice of Assessment on the Landlord and the Tenant confirming the amount the Landlord must pay the Tenant which notice should be dated, give the date of the valuation and detail how the valuer arrived at the values and amounts.

Either the Landlord or the Tenant can appeal the Notice of Assessment to the Lands Tribunal within 21 days. The Tenant may also withdraw the Notice of Intention to Relinquish within 35 days of the Notice of Assessment or 14 days after the Lands Tribunal's decision on appeal.

The Landlord has to decide how to react to the Notice of Assessment within 28 days of the last date on which the Tenant could withdraw the Notice of Intention to Relinquish, ie 35 days after the Notice of Assessment is received.

Notice of Acceptance

The Landlord can serve a Notice of Acceptance on the Tenant stating that the Landlord will pay to the Tenant the amount assessed by the valuer, payment being made within 6 months of that date. The Landlord can withdraw the Notice of Acceptance at any time before the compensation is paid. Payment of the compensation amount terminates the Tenancy.

Notice of Declinature

Alternatively, the Landlord can serve a Notice of Declinature.

Where the Landlord serves a Notice of Declinature, fails to serve a Notice of Acceptance timeously or serves but then withdraws a Notice of Acceptance, the Tenant may assign the tenancy to a new entrant to farming or a person who is progressing in farming.

Assignation

The Tenant must complete the assignation within one year of receiving the Notice of Declinature or the date when the time limit to serve a Notice of Acceptance has passed, the date the withdrawal of the Notice of Acceptance is intimated or where the Landlord fails to pay the compensation the date falling on the last date for payment.

The Landlord may object to the proposed assignation if the proposed assignee is not an individual who is a new entrant to farming or who is progressing in farming or the Landlord has reasonable grounds for objecting. Reasonable grounds include but are not limited to, the Landlord not being satisfied that the proposed assignee would have the ability to pay the rent due under the lease or for adequate maintenance of the land or had skills or experience required to manage and maintain the land in accordance with the rules of good husbandry.

The ground of objection that the proposed assignee lacks the skills or experience required does not apply where the proposed assignee is a new entrant to farming and is engaged or will begin within 6 months a course of relevant training in agriculture which he or she is expected to complete satisfactorily within 4 years and that person has made arrangements to ensure the holding is farmed with reasonable efficiency until the course is completed.

CHAPTER FOURTEEN

SUCCESSION

The Tenant's right to bequeath a tenancy to successors or the executors' right to transfer the tenancy on intestacy is a hallmark of agricultural tenancies. It is an area of law with very strict time limits and can cause considerable difficulty in practice.

1991 Act Tenancies

Succession to 1991 Act tenancies is covered by s11 and s12. These provisions apply to both leases in writing and unwritten leases.

Once it has been established by the executors that the deceased person was the tenant of an agricultural holding to which the 1991 Act applies, the next question is whether there is a bequest of the lease in the deceased's will.

Testate Succession

s11 states a tenant may bequeath his interest in the tenancy to any person within a list of eligible legatees defined in s1A. This has to be done by a specific bequest - "I bequeath the tenancy of Whiteknowes Farm to my son Hugh...".

The list of potentially eligible legatees contains a wide range of relatives both by blood and marriage. Within this list of legatees is a privileged group known as the "near relatives" as defined in s10(A) (6).

The bequest must be to one person only. If there is no specific bequest the lease does not fall into the residue of the estate, it falls into intestacy. The residuary beneficiary is not entitled to succeed to the lease where there is no specific legacy.

If there is a written lease then the executors should check whether that lease prohibited successors. If so, the executors are faced with a dilemma. The lease prohibits bequests but the tenant has made a bequest – should the executors act on that bequest and hope the Landlord does not realise it is invalid or should they assume the bequest was unlawful from the start and ignore it? I would tend to recommend that the executors should treat the bequest as valid and follow the s11 procedure because, as we will see below, there is the possibility that the Landlord does not challenge the bequest, and even if a successful challenge is made, the executors have a second chance to transfer the tenancy.

In terms of s11 (2) the legatee has to give notice to the Landlord within 21 days of the tenant's death. That is a very tight timescale within which to investigate whether there was a tenancy, whether the deceased bequeathed the tenancy in his or her will and then to take instructions from the legatee as to whether they wish to accept the bequest and if so to draft the notice and intimate it on the Landlord. The only exception to this time limit is where the legatee can show that he or she has been prevented from giving notice by "some unavoidable cause", ie severe illness. If the legatee does not accept the bequest the lease does not come to an end but the right to the lease is treated as intestate estate.

The Landlord has 30 days from receipt of the notice to object to the proposed legatee by serving a counter-notice intimating that the Landlord objects to receiving the legatee as the tenant under the lease. If the legatee is a "near relative" of the deceased the Landlord can only object under s12A(3) on the grounds that the legatee is not of good character, does not have sufficient resources to allow the person to farm the holding with reasonable efficiency or does not have sufficient training in agriculture or sufficient practical experience of farming to farm the holding with reasonable efficiency. This last ground of objection does not apply where the legatee is engaged in, or will begin within 6 months of the notice being given, a course of relevant training in agriculture which the person is expected satisfactorily to complete within 4 years from the date of the notice and in the meantime has arranged for the holding to be farmed with reasonable efficiency until the person completes that course.

If the Landlord serves a counter-notice he or she must follow up with a referral to the Land Court within one month of the date of the counter-notice. Where the Landlord fails to make such a referral to the Land Court the counter-notice ceases to have effect and the lease is binding on the legatee.

If the Landlord does make a referral to the Land Court and the court believes any ground of objection by the Landlord has been established then the Land Court must make an order declaring the bequest to be null and void.

If the legatee is not a "near relative" but one of the wider list of eligible legatees the Landlord can serve a counter-notice as above without giving any reason and within one month of the date of the counter-notice apply to the Land Court. Under s12B the onus of proof is reversed so the legatee must make the case and prove to the satisfaction of the Land Court that there is a "reasonable ground" for not declaring the bequest to be null and void. Thus it can be seen that the near relative legatee is in a much stronger position.

Intestate Succession

Intestacy in agricultural law is not the same as intestacy under the general law. The rules on intestacy apply where there is no will, where there is a will but there is no specific bequest of the tenancy, where there was a specific bequest but the legatee rejected the bequest and where there was a specific bequest but it was declared null and void by the Land Court under s12A or s12B. These provisions are found in S16 of the Succession Scotland Act 1964. Where a legatee's intimation has been challenged by the Landlord and that challenge was successful the lease is not terminated. The executors have a second chance to deal with the tenancy under intestacy.

The executors confirm to the tenancy and then transfer it to an acquirer who then intimates to the Landlord. That whole process must be completed within one year of the date of death. During that period of one year from the date of death the executors can pay the rent as executors and this can safely be accepted by the Landlord without compromising the Landlord's ability to challenge the eventual acquirer. As with legacies, there can be only one acquirer.

The executor can nominate any person as an acquirer but the Landlord's consent is required where the acquirer is not a person entitled to succeed to the deceased's intestate estate or claim legal rights or prior rights on the deceased's estate.

The acquirer must intimate to the Landlord that he or she has acquired the tenancy within 21 days of the acquisition. The Landlord has the same opportunity to object to a near relative acquirer under s12A and any other acquirer under s12B and the same provisions for referral to the Land Court apply.

A Tenant making a will must consider very carefully whether or not to make a specific bequest of the tenancy. A bequest might be prohibited by the lease or the legatee might fail to take the necessary action within 21 days of the Tenant's death. It may be preferable to allow the tenancy to fall into intestacy because the time limit of one year from date of death to transfer the tenancy to an acquirer is much longer. If a Tenant would rather allow the tenancy to fall into intestacy but wants to give his or her executors some direction an expression of wish could be drafted as part of the will or as a separate testamentary writing. It must be made clear that the expression of wish is not a bequest, eg "Without making any specific bequest of my tenancy of Whiteknowes Farm I express the wish that my executors consider transferring the said tenancy to my son Hugh".

Joint Tenants

It is not unusual for leases to be granted to more than one tenant or for other tenants to be added to leases. If that is the case then the interest of the deceased person might pass on survivorship or the tenancy might be held by two or more tenants in pro indiviso shares. If the lease was in favour of X and Y and the survivor and X dies then Y becomes the sole tenant but if the lease was in favour of X and Y with no survivorship destination then when X dies his executors have to deal with a pro indiviso interest in the tenancy so all of the above applies but instead of referring to the tenancy as a whole the reference is to a pro indiviso share.

SLDTs, LDTs, MLDTs and Repairing Leases

The modern forms of agricultural tenancy are also capable of being transferred on the death of the original tenant. As these tenancies have a fixed duration their value to a legatee or acquirer is less than a 1991 Act tenancy. The procedure the executors should follow is similar to the above and is set out in sections s20, s21 and s22 of the 2003 Act.

S21 of the 2003 Act provides that a Tenant may bequeath the tenancy and applies the same definition of eligible legatees and near relatives as apply to 1991 Act tenancies. The legatee must give notice to the Landlord of the bequest within 21 days of the death of the Tenant. The Landlord can serve a counter-notice objecting to the Tenant within one month of receiving the notice. The grounds of objection are the same in relation to near relatives and other persons as those for 1991 Act tenancies.

S16 of the 1964 Act is specifically applied to SLDTs, LDTs, MLDTs and Repairing Tenancies by s20 of the 2003 Act. The executors of the deceased tenant can transfer the tenancy on "intestacy", ie where there is legal intestacy, where there is no specific bequest of the tenancy, where the legatee rejects the bequest or where the bequest is declared null and void. The executors transfer the tenancy to the person they have selected and that person must give notice to the Landlord within 21 days of the transfer.

The Landlord can object to the transfer and apply to the Land Court on the same grounds as he or she could have objected to the transfer of a 1991 Act tenancy. However, in relation to 2003 Act tenancies the Landlord has another potential course of action. The executors can transfer the tenancy to any person but where that person is not a person who would have been entitled to inherit the deceased's estate on intestacy or claim legal rights or prior rights in relation to that estate then the Landlord can give notice under s22(3) within 30 days of receiving the notice of transfer that he or she intends to acquire the tenant's interest in the lease.

The 2003 Act imposes a limit on the discretion of the executors to choose a potential successor to the lease on intestacy. Any transfer of the lease must be in "the best interests of the deceased's estate."

Partnership Leases

Succession to these tenancies depends on the terms of the partnership agreement. Some end on the death of the general partner and some allow for assignation of the general partner's interest. S72 of the 2003 Act provides that if the Landlord tries to terminate the lease by terminating the partnership (meaning the Tenant no longer exists) then the general partner can become a secure Tenant as an individual if the notice procedure is followed. That section does not apply if the partnership ends because the Tenant dies, only if the Landlord does something to terminate the partnership. That means that if the partnership agreement terminates on the death of the general partner then s72 will not save the tenancy.

CHAPTER FIFTEEN

TERMINATION

We have seen that 1991 Act tenancies can pass down through generations of the same family and that tacit relocation automatically applies to all such leases.

This chapter deals with the limited circumstances in which a Landlord can terminate a 1991 Act tenancy and also the ways in which SLDTs, LDTs, MLDTs and Repairing Tenancies are terminated.

1991 Act Tenancies

A 1991 Act tenancy can only be terminated by a notice which complies with s21 of the 1991 Act. Notices covered by this section can be given by the Landlord to the Tenant, in which case they are referred to as Notices to Quit or by a Tenant to a Landlord in which case they are referred to as Notices of Intention to Quit. Any such notice must be in writing and given more than one year but less than two years before the date of termination or the date of continuation under tacit relocation.

Where a Notice to Quit is served the Tenant can, under s22 of the 1991 Act, serve a counter-notice in writing on the Landlord within one month from the date of the notice to quit. The counter-notice states that the Tenant is invoking s22 and the Notice to Quit shall not have effect unless the Land Court consents to the operation of the notice.

There are some exceptions to s22 and these are found in s22(2) and include for example where the tenancy is terminated because the

Tenant had failed to comply with a notice from the Landlord requiring the Tenant within 2 months to pay any rent due in respect of the holding or where the Tenant is not farming in accordance with the rules of good husbandry. In this latter case the Landlord can apply to the Land Court before serving the Notice to Quit under s26 of the 1991 Act for a certificate of bad husbandry. Even within the scope of these limited exceptions the Tenant can still give notice to the Landlord within 30 days that the Tenant requires any question relating to a notice which falls within s22(2) to be determined by the Land Court.

An application by the Landlord to the Land Court for consent to the operation of the Notice to Quit must be made within one month after service of the counter notice. If the result of the Tenant's referral of a question relating to a notice falling within s22(2) is that s22(1) should in fact have applied to the notice the Tenant has one month from the date of the Land Court's determination to serve a counter notice.

The Land Court must consent to the operation of the Notice to Quit if the Court is satisfied that any one or more of the following matters specified in the Landlord's application are established:-

- that the carrying out of the purpose for which the Landlord proposes to terminate the tenancy is desirable in the interests of good husbandry as respects the land to which the notice relates treated as a separate unit

- that the carrying out thereof is desirable in the interests of good management of the estate of which that land consists or forms part

- that the carrying out thereof is desirable for the purposes of agricultural research, education, experiment or demonstration or for the purposes of the enactments relating to allotments or small holdings

- that greater hardship would be caused by withholding rather than giving consent to the operation of the notice

- that the Landlord proposes to terminate the tenancy for the purpose of the land being used for a use other than agriculture.

Even where the Land Court are so satisfied, they must withhold consent if it appears that a fair and reasonable Landlord would not insist on possession or where the use of the land proposed by the Landlord would not create greater economic and social benefits to the community than would exist if the tenancy were not terminated.

If the Land Court do consent to the operation of a Notice to Quit then they may attach conditions to secure that the land to which the notice relates will be used for the purpose for which the Landlord proposes to terminate the tenancy.

Short Limited Duration Tenancies

SLDTs terminate at their stated end date. There is no requirement to serve a notice to quit but it is good practice to do so as the serving of a notice to quit negates any argument that the Landlord has consented to the Tenant remaining in occupation.

Where the Tenant remains in occupation with the consent of the Landlord the SLDT continues for a total maximum of 5 years from the original start date. If the Tenant continues in occupation with the consent of the Landlord beyond the maximum 5-year period for an SLDT then the tenancy converts to become an MLDT for 10 years from the original start date of the SLDT.

Limited Duration Tenancies

No new LDTs can be created but as there are still many in existence so the provisions on termination remain relevant.

A Limited Duration tenancy is terminated by the Landlord giving the Tenant two notices. The first notice must be served more than two years but less than three years before the termination date and must advise the Tenant that the Landlord intents to terminate the tenancy on the termination date. The second notice must be served more than one year but less than two years before the termination date and must state that the Tenant shall quit the land at the termination date. There must be a period of at least 90 days between the service of these two notices.

If the Landlord fails to serve these notices then the provisions of s8 (6) of the 2003 apply. These detail a series of statutory continuations in a cycle of three years being a first short continuation, three years being a second short continuation and ten years being a long continuation. This cycle of continuations can be repeated without limit. There are detailed provisions on how notices should be given during the periods of continuation.

The Landlord and the Tenant can agree at any time to terminate an LDT provided the agreement is in writing, entered into after the commencement of the tenancy and provides for any compensation payable by the Landlord or the Tenant to the other.

Modern Limited Duration Tenancies

Similar provisions apply to MLDTs which can also be terminated by agreement in writing entered into after the commencement of the tenancy and providing for any compensation payable by the Landlord or the Tenant to the other.

S8B of the 2003 Act as amended by the 2016 Act provides for the same double notice procedure to terminate MLDTs. A notice of intention to terminate the tenancy must be given by the Landlord to the Tenant more than two years but less than three years before the termination date and this must be followed up by a notice to quit served more than one year but less than two years before the termination date with at least 90 days between the service of the two notices.

The Tenant can terminate an MLDT by giving notice in writing to the Landlord of his or her intention to do so more than one year but less than two years before the termination date.

Where the MLDT contains a break clause (where the Tenant is a new entrant to farming) either the Landlord or the Tenant can terminate the lease at the break by giving notice in writing to the other more than one year but less than two years before the break date. The Landlord may only serve such a notice where the Tenant is not using the Land in accordance with the rules of good husbandry or is otherwise failing to comply with any other provisions of the lease. The Tenant can give notice without giving reasons.

If the MLDT continues after the termination date with neither party having taken any action to terminate the lease the tenancy continues for a further term of 7 years but can be terminated during that continuation by either party serving notice as above.

The Landlord and the Tenant can agree in writing to extend the term of the MLDT.

Repairing Tenancies

Once enacted, s94 of the 2016 Act will introduce s8F and s8G to the 2003 Act and will provide that the ss8A to 8C on termination of MLDTs apply to Repairing Tenancies.

Where a Repairing Tenancy has a break clause (where the Tenant is a new entrant to farming) the Tenant can give notice to terminate the tenancy at any time during the repairing period provided that the notice is in writing, specifies the date to quit which must be within the repairing period and must be given more than one year but less than two years before the date specified in the notice. The Tenant does not need to give reasons for giving notice. The Landlord can also serve notice to terminate the tenancy during the repairing period. The notice must be in writing, state that the Tenant must quit the land on the expiry of the repairing period and be given more than one year but less than two years before the expiry of the repairing period. The notice must give the Landlord's reasons for terminating the tenancy and those reasons cannot include the ground that the Tenant is not farming the land in accordance with the rules of good husbandry.

CHAPTER SIXTEEN

THE SCOTTISH LAND COURT

The Scottish Land Court has jurisdiction to decide disputes regarding many of the issues dealt with in the earlier chapters of this book.

Constitution

The Court comprises a Chairman, a deputy chairman and two agricultural members. The court also has jurisdiction in crofting matters so one of the court members must be a Gaelic speaker.

The website for the court is www.scottish-land-court.org.uk and it has details of the rules of court and a data base of decisions.

The procedure for raising an action and all the necessary forms are found on the website. The rules are in general less formal than the normal Sheriff Court or Court of Session rules the idea being that individuals should be able to resolve disputes in the Land Court themselves without recourse to solicitors. In reality most litigants instruct a solicitor and often an advocate as well.

The procedure starts with one party filling in a written application form and serving it on the other party to the dispute. The court will determine the best way to deal with the case; either by written pleadings or by a proof. The court staff convey the court's decision on how the case should proceed and give the relevant time limits, eg the deadline for the defender to respond, a period of adjustment and the date when the written pleadings are final.

The court will then consider the written pleadings and possibly require a hearing. After any hearing the court gives a written decision and the decision is reported on the website.

Jurisdiction – 1991 Act Tenancies

Historically disputes were resolved by arbitration between the Landlord and the Tenant but the 2003 Act amended s60 of the 1991 Act to give the Land Court a wide jurisdiction over:-

- whether a tenancy of an agricultural holding exists or has been terminated
- any question or difference between the Landlord and the Tenant of such a holding arising out of the tenancy or in connection with the holding, whether such a question arises during the currency of or after the termination of the tenancy
- any claim by the Landlord or the Tenant of such a holding against the other which arises under the 1991 Act or under any rule of law, custom or agreement, or out of the termination of the tenancy or part thereof
- any other issue of fact or law relating to a tenancy of such a holding or any other type of agricultural tenancy or agriculture which the Landlord or Tenant reasonably require to have resolved.

S116 of the Land Reform (Scotland) Act 2016 gives the Land Court jurisdiction on an application by the Tenant to approve or withhold approval in respect of any improvement notified to the Landlord by the Tenant by way of an amnesty notice to which the Landlord has objected.

Jurisdiction is expressly excluded in respect of any question as to who is entitled to succeed to the estate of a deceased person on intestacy and the validity of any bequest or any transfer of an interest under the lease or whether any such transfer is in the best interests of the estate of a deceased person. These matters must be resolved in the Sherriff Court or the Court of Session.

It remains open to the Landlord and the Tenant to agree to refer some disputes to arbitration rather than to the Land Court. Matters which cannot be referred to arbitration include disputes regarding s11 (notices of bequest), s12 (transfer of a lease on intestacy), s22 (restrictions on operation of notices to quit) and s26 (certificates of bad husbandry).

Jurisdiction – 2003 Act Tenancies

S77 of the 2003 Act gives the Land Court jurisdiction to hear and determine:-

- whether a Short Limited Duration Tenancy, a Limited Duration Tenancy, a Modern Limited Duration Tenancy, a Repairing Tenancy or a grazing lease exists or has been terminated

- any question or difference between the Landlord and the Tenant arising out of or in connection with any such tenancy whether the question or difference arises during the currency of or on or after the termination of the tenancy

- any claim by the Landlord or the Tenant of any such tenancy against the other which arises by virtue of the 2003 Act or under any rule of law, custom or agreement, on or out of the termination of the tenancy or any part of it

- any other issue of fact or law relating to any such tenancy or a 1991 Act tenancy or agriculture which the Landlord and the Tenant reasonably require to have resolved.

As with 1991 Act tenancies jurisdiction is excluded in respect of any question as to who is entitled to succeed to the estate of a deceased person on intestacy or the validity of any bequest or any transfer of any interest under the lease constituting the tenancy or whether any such transfer is in the best interests of the estate of the deceased person.

The parties may agree to refer their dispute to arbitration rather than to the Land Court unless the dispute is regarding s21 (notices of bequest) or s22 (transfer of a lease on intestacy).

Remedies

The Land Court may make or grant any or all of the following orders:-

- a decree of interdict, including interim interdict
- an order *ad factum praestandum* or an order of specific implement including in both cases an interim order
- an order of specific restitution
- an order of reduction or rectification
- an order of removal or ejection, but not an interim order
- an order for damages or other substitutionary redress
- a declarator

If an order *ad factum praestandum* or an order of specific implement is made against a Landlord in relation to a failure of the Landlord to fulfil any obligation to the Tenant in respect of fixed equipment the Land Court must specify the date by which the Landlord is to comply with the order but may on application by the Landlord specify a later date if satisfied that the Landlord intends to comply with the order but reasonably requires more time to do so.

Any decision of the Land Court can be appealed to the Court of Session.

CHAPTER SEVENTEEN

THE TENANT FARMING COMMISSIONER

The role of the Tenant Farming Commissioner was created by the Land Reform (Scotland) Act 2016.

Functions

The stated functions of the Commissioner are:-

- to prepare codes of practice on agricultural holdings
- to promote those codes of practice
- to prepare a report on the operation of agents of Landlords and Tenants
- to prepare recommendations for a modern list of improvements to agricultural holdings
- to refer for the opinion of the Land Court any question of law relating to agricultural holdings
- to collaborate with the Scottish Land Commissioners to the extent that their functions relate to agriculture and agricultural holdings
- to exercise any other functions conferred on the Commissioner by any enactment

The Commissioner is directed to exercise those functions *"with a view to encouraging good relations between landlords and tenants of agricultural holdings"*.

Codes of Practice

The Commissioner is empowered to produce codes of practice about rent reviews, Tenant's improvements, conduct of agents, fulfilling the obligations of Landlord and Tenant, succession and assignation, compensation at waygo, negotiating the terms of Modern Limited Duration Tenancies and Repairing Tenancies, managing sporting leases and game management.

The Land Reform (Scotland) Bill 2024 adds to that list power to make codes of practice on the use of land for non-agricultural purposes.

The Commissioner has to date published 7 codes of practice and 2 reviews. The statutorily required review on the operation of agents of Landlords and Tenants was published in April 2018 and a review of Buccleugh Estate's Agricultural Tenancy Negotiations was published in July 2018.

The codes of practice cover:-

- Agreeing and Managing Agricultural Leases
- Amnesty on Tenant's Improvements
- Late Payment of Rent
- Planning the Future of Limited Partnerships
- Sporting Rights

- Maintenance of the Condition of Tenanted Agricultural Holdings
- Conducting Rent Reviews

The Commissioner is to promote the observance of these codes of practice by educating and advising about the codes, supporting best practice in accordance with the codes among Landlords and Tenants of agricultural holdings and their agents, working in collaboration with other persons and contributing to the development and delivery of policies and strategies in relation to agricultural holdings.

Breach of Code of Practice

If someone believes there has been a breach of a code of practice that person can apply to the Tenant Farming Commissioner to inquire into the alleged breach if that person has a relevant interest in the tenancy or would have an interest in the relevant tenancy but for the alleged breach.

The Tenant Farming Commissioner may inquire into an alleged breach only if satisfied that the applicant has an interest in the tenancy or would do but for the alleged breach, the application contains sufficient information and the application is not based on substantially the same facts as a previous application from the same applicant.

The Commissioner can request further information from the applicant. If the application does not meet the above conditions, a request for further information has been made and that information has not been forthcoming within any time limit set or the Commissioner believes that a request for further information would not provide sufficient information to proceed the Commissioner may dismiss the application by giving notice in writing to the applicant.

Inquiry

If the Commissioner proceeds with the inquiry he or she must give notice to the applicant and each person with an interest in the relevant tenancy, send a copy of the application to each of those persons and require a response from them by the end of such period as the Commissioner may specify.

The Commissioner has power to impose a fine of up to £1,000, a "non-compliance penalty", if any person fails to provide such a response or fails to respond to a requirement to provide information to the Commissioner.

Report

As soon as reasonably practicable after an inquiry into an alleged breach the Commissioner must publish a report setting out the Commissioner's decision as to whether the code has been breached, the reasoning for reaching that decision, the relevant facts on which the decision is based and such recommendations as the Commissioner considers appropriate. The Commissioner can alternatively find that there is not sufficient information for the Commissioner to reach a decision on breach of the code of practice.

CHAPTER EIGHTEEN

USEFUL DEFINITIONS

The following words have specific statutory definitions:-

"**agriculture**" includes horticulture, fruit growing; seed growing; dairy farming; livestock breeding and keeping; the use of land as grazing land, meadow land, osier land, market gardens and nursery grounds; and the use of land for woodlands whether that use is ancillary to the farming of land for other agricultural purposes: and "agricultural" shall be construed accordingly *s85 1991 Act*

"**agricultural holding**" means the aggregate of the agricultural land comprised in a lease, not being a lease under which the land is let to the tenant during his continuation in any office, appointment or employment held under the landlord *s1 1991 Act*

"**agricultural land**" means land used for agriculture for the purposes of a trade or business *s1 1991 Act*

"**fixed equipment**" includes any building or structure affixed to land and any works on, in, over or under land, and also includes anything grown on land for a purpose other than use after severance from the land, consumption of the thing grown or of produce thereof, or amenity, and, without prejudice to the foregoing generality, includes the following things, that is to say –

- all permanent buildings, including farm houses and farm cottages, necessary for the proper conduct of the agricultural holding;

- all permanent fences, including hedges, stone dykes, gate posts and gates
- all ditches, open drains and tile drains, conduits and culverts, ponds, sluices, flood banks and main water courses;
- stells, fanks, folds, dippers, pens and bughts necessary for the proper conduct of the holding;
- farm access or service roads, bridges and fords;
- water and sewerage systems;
- electrical installations including generating plant, fixed motors, wiring systems, switches and plug sockets;
- shelter belts

and references to fixed equipment on land shall be construed accordingly *s85 1991 Act*

"**landlord**" means (one) any person for the time being entitled to receive the rents and profits or to take possession of an agricultural holding, and includes the executor, assignee, legatee, disponee, guardian, curator bonis or tutor of a landlord or the trustee or interim trustee in the sequestration of a landlord's estate *s85 1991 Act* or (two) any person for the time being entitled to receive the rents under a lease constituting a tenancy and includes the executor, assignee, legatee, disponee, guardian or legal representative (within the meaning of Part I of the Children (Scotland) Act 1995 (c.36) of a landlord or the trustee or interim trustee in the sequestration under the Bankruptcy (Scotland) Act 2016, of a landlord's estate *s93 2003 Act* "**lease**" means a letting of land for a term of years, or for lives, or for lives and years or from year to year *s85 1991 Act*

"**livestock**" means any creature kept for the production of food, wool, skins or fur or for the purpose of its use in the farming of land *s85 1991 Act*

"**near relative**" in relation to a tenant of an agricultural holding means-

- a parent of the tenant
- a spouse or civil partner of the tenant
- a child of the tenant
- a spouse or civil partner of such a child
- a grandchild of the tenant
- a brother or sister of the tenant
- a spouse or civil partner of such a brother or sister
- a child of a brother or sister of the tenant
- a grandchild of the brother or sister of the tenant
- a brother or sister of the tenant's spouse or civil partner
- a spouse or civil partner of such brother or sister
- a child of such a brother or sister

- a grandchild or such a brother or sister

"**produce**" means anything (whether live or dead) produced in the course of agriculture *s85 1991 Act*

"**tenant**" means (one) the holder of land under a lease of an agricultural holding and includes the executor, assignee, legatee, disponee, guardian, tutor or curator bonis of a tenant or the trustee or interim trustee in the sequestration of a tenant's estate *s85 1991 Act* or (two) the holder of land under a tenancy constituted by a lease and includes the executor, assignee, legatee, disponee, guardian or legal representative (within the meaning of Part I of the Children (Scotland) Act 1995) of a tenant or the trustee or interim trustee in the sequestration, under the Bankruptcy (Scotland) Act 2016 of a tenant's estate *s93 2003 Act*

The rules of good estate management and the rules of good husbandry are defined in the Agriculture (Scotland) Act 1948.

Good Estate Management

Schedule 5 defines good estate management as shown below.

> For the purposes of this Act, the owner of agricultural land shall be deemed to fulfil his responsibilities to manage it in accordance with the rules of good estate management in so far as his management of the land and (so far as it affects the management of that land) of other land managed by him is such as to be reasonably adequate, having regard to the character and situation of the land and other relevant circumstances, to enable an occupier of the land reasonably skilled in husbandry to maintain efficient production as respects both the kind of produce and the quality and quantity thereof. In determining whether the management

> of land is such as aforesaid regard shall be had, but without prejudice to the generality of the provisions of the last foregoing paragraph, to the extent to which the owner is making regular muirburn in the interests of sheep stock, exercising systematic control of vermin on land not in the control of a tenant, and undertaking the eradication of bracken, whins and broom so far as is reasonably practicable, and to the extent to which the owner is fulfilling his responsibilities in relation to the provision, improvement, replacement and renewal of the fixed equipment on the land in so far as is necessary to enable an occupier reasonably skilled in husbandry to maintain efficient, production as aforesaid.
>
> If enacted, the Land Reform (Scotland) Bill 2024 would add the words "sustainable and regenerative" after the word "efficient" in the above definition.

Good Husbandry

Schedule 6 defines good husbandry as shown below.

> For the purposes of this Act, the occupier of an agricultural unit shall be deemed to fulfil his responsibilities to farm it in accordance with the rules of good husbandry in so far as the extent to which and the manner in which the unit is being farmed (as respects both the kind of operations carried out and the way in which they are carried out) are such that, having regard to the character and situation of the unit, the standard of management thereof by the owner and other relevant circumstances, the occupier is maintaining a reasonable standard of efficient production, as respects both the kind of produce and the quality and quantity thereof, while keeping the unit in a condition to enable such a standard to be maintained in the future.

In determining whether the manner in which a unit is being farmed is such as aforesaid regard shall be had, but without prejudice to the generality of the provisions of the last foregoing paragraph, to the following:—

(a) the maintenance of permanent grassland (whether meadow or pasture) properly mown or grazed and in a good state of cultivation and fertility;

(b) the handling or cropping of the arable land, including the treatment of temporary grass, so as to maintain it clean and in a good state of cultivation and fertility;

(c) where the system of farming practised requires the keeping of livestock, the proper stocking of the holding;

(d) the maintenance of an efficient standard of management of livestock;

(e) as regards hill sheep farming in particular:—

(i) the maintenance of a sheep stock of a suitable breed and type in regular ages (so far as is reasonably possible) and the keeping and management thereof in accordance with the recognised practices of hill sheep farming;

(ii) the use of lug, horn or other stock marks means of identifying animals for the purpose of determining ownership of stock sheep;

(iii) the regular selection and retention of the best female stock for breeding;

(iv) the regular selection and use of tups possessing the qualities most suitable and desirable for the flock;

(v) the extent to which regular muirburn is made;

(f) the extent to which the necessary steps are being taken—

(i) to secure and maintain the freedom of crops and livestock from disease and from infestation by insects and other pests;

(ii) to exercise systematic control of vermin and of bracken, whins, broom and injurious weeds;

(iii) to protect and preserve crops harvested or in course of being harvested;

(iv) to carry out necessary work of maintenance and repair of the fixed and other equipment.

If enacted, the Land Reform (Scotland) Bill 2024 would add the words "sustainable and regenerative" after the word "efficient" in the above definition. The Bill would also add the health and wellbeing of livestock as a further consideration to be taken into account in assessing whether the holding was being farmed in accordance with the rules of good husbandry.

MORE BOOKS BY LAW BRIEF PUBLISHING

A selection of our other titles available now:-

'A Practical Guide to Probation Breaches and Other Applications' by Mark Thomas
'A Practical Guide to Remarriage and Divorce' by Cordelia Williams & Claire Howard
'A Practical Guide to Privacy, Transparency, Reporting Restrictions and Closed Proceedings in the Court of Protection' by Laura Mannering
'Beaumont on Barristers – A Guide to Defending Disciplinary Proceedings (Second Edition)' by Marc Beaumont
'A Practical Guide to Payments for Environmental Services' by Ben Sharples
'A Practical Guide to the Law of Pregnancy and Maternity at Work' by Rebecca Thomas
'A Practical Guide to Redundancy – Second Edition' by Philip Hyland & Collette Moore
'A Practical Guide to International Issues for Scottish Family Lawyers' by Susie Mountain, Donna McKay, Ken MacDonald
'A Practical Guide to the Law on Deprivation of Liberty' by Ben Troke
'A Practical Guide to Rights over Airspace and Subsoil – Second Edition' by Daniel Gatty
'A Practical Guide to the Law in Relation to Inquests' by Ramya Nagesh
'A Practical Guide to the Construction and Rectification of Wills and Trust Instruments (Second Edition)' by Edward Hewitt
'A Practical Guide to Data Protection in Social Housing' by Clare Paterson
'A Practical Guide to Spousal Maintenance – Second Edition' by Liz Cowell
'A Practical Guide to International Parental Child Abduction Law (England and Wales)' by Dr Onyója Momoh
'A Practical Guide to Deprivation of British Citizenship' by Sean Ell
'A Practical Guide to Commercial Property Service Charges' by Rachel Garton
'A Practical Guide to Clinical Negligence – Third Edition' by Geoffrey Simpson-Scott (Geoff)
'A Practical Guide to the Rights of Grandparents in Children Proceedings – Second Edition' by Stuart Barlow

'The Electronic Communications Code: A Practical Guide – Second Edition' by Kerry Bretherton KC, James Castle, Mark Loveday
'A Practical Guide to the Independent School Standards – September 2023 Edition' by Sarah McKimm
'A Practical Guide to Estate Administration and Crypto Assets' by Richard Marshall
'A Practical Guide to Parental Alienation in Private and Public Law Children Cases' by Sam King QC & Frankie Shama
'Contested Heritage – Removing Art from Land and Historic Buildings' by Richard Harwood QC, Catherine Dobson, David Sawtell
'The Limits of Separate Legal Personality: When Those Running a Company Can Be Held Personally Liable for Losses Caused to Third Parties Outside of the Company' by Dr Mike Wilkinson
'A Practical Guide to Transgender Law' by Robin Moira White & Nicola Newbegin
'A Practical Guide to 'Stranded Spouses' in Family Law' by Mani Singh Basi
'A Practical Guide to Residential Freehold Conveyancing' by Lorraine Richardson
'A Practical Guide to Pensions on Divorce for Lawyers' by Bryan Scant
'A Practical Guide to Challenging Sham Marriage Allegations in Immigration Law' by Priya Solanki
'A Practical Guide to Digital Communications Evidence in Criminal Law' by Sam Willis
'A Practical Guide to Legal Rights in Scotland' by Sarah-Jane Macdonald
'A Practical Guide to New Build Conveyancing' by Paul Sams & Rebecca East
'A Practical Guide to Inherited Wealth on Divorce' by Hayley Trim
'A Practical Guide to Practice Direction 12J and Domestic Abuse in Private Law Children Proceedings' by Rebecca Cross & Malvika Jaganmohan
'A Practical Guide to Confiscation and Restraint' by Narita Bahra QC, John Carl Townsend, David Winch
'A Practical Guide to the Law of Forests in Scotland' by Philip Buchan
'A Practical Guide to Health and Medical Cases in Immigration Law' by Rebecca Chapman & Miranda Butler
'A Practical Guide to Bad Character Evidence for Criminal Practitioners by Aparna Rao
'A Practical Guide to Extradition Law post-Brexit' by Myles Grandison et al
'A Practical Guide to Hoarding and Mental Health for Housing Lawyers' by Rachel Coyle

'Stephens on Contractual Indemnities' by Richard Stephens

'A Practical Guide to the EU Succession Regulation' by Richard Frimston

'A Practical Guide to Solicitor and Client Costs – Second Edition' by Robin Dunne

'Constructive Dismissal – Practice Pointers and Principles' by Benjimin Burgher

'A Practical Guide to Religion and Belief Discrimination Claims in the Workplace' by Kashif Ali

'A Practical Guide to the Law of Medical Treatment Decisions' by Ben Troke

'Fundamental Dishonesty and QOCS in Personal Injury Proceedings: Law and Practice' by Jake Rowley

'A Practical Guide to the Law in Relation to School Exclusions' by Charlotte Hadfield & Alice de Coverley

'A Practical Guide to Divorce for the Silver Separators' by Karin Walker

'The Right to be Forgotten – The Law and Practical Issues' by Melissa Stock

'A Practical Guide to Planning Law and Rights of Way in National Parks, the Broads and AONBs' by James Maurici QC, James Neill et al

'A Practical Guide to Election Law' by Tom Tabori

'A Practical Guide to the Law in Relation to Surrogacy' by Andrew Powell

'A Practical Guide to Claims Arising from Fatal Accidents – Second Edition' by James Patience

'A Practical Guide to Asbestos Claims' by Jonathan Owen & Gareth McAloon

'A Practical Guide to Stamp Duty Land Tax in England and Northern Ireland' by Suzanne O'Hara

'A Practical Guide to the Law of Farming Partnerships' by Philip Whitcomb

'A Practical Guide to the Law of Unlawful Eviction and Harassment – Second Edition' by Stephanie Lovegrove

'A Practical Guide to Costs in Personal Injury Claims – Second Edition' by Matthew Hoe

'A Practical Guide to the General Data Protection Regulation (GDPR) – Second Edition' by Keith Markham

'A Practical Guide to Working with Litigants in Person and McKenzie Friends in Family Cases' by Stuart Barlow

'Protecting Unregistered Brands: A Practical Guide to the Law of Passing Off' by Lorna Brazell

'A Practical Guide to Secondary Liability and Joint Enterprise Post-Jogee' by Joanne Cecil & James Mehigan

'A Practical Guide to the Pre-Action RTA Claims Protocol for Personal Injury Lawyers' by Antonia Ford

'A Practical Guide to Neighbour Disputes and the Law' by Alexander Walsh

'A Practical Guide to Coercive Control for Legal Practitioners and Victims' by Rachel Horman

'A Practical Guide to the Law of Driverless Cars – Second Edition'

by Alex Glassbrook, Emma Northey & Scarlett Milligan

'A Practical Guide to TOLATA Claims' by Greg Williams

'A Practical Guide to Elderly Law – Second Edition' by Justin Patten

'A Practical Guide to Responding to Housing Disrepair and Unfitness Claims' by Iain Wightwick

'A Practical Guide to the Law of Bullying and Harassment in the Workplace' by Philip Hyland

'How to Be a Freelance Solicitor: A Practical Guide to the SRA-Regulated Freelance Solicitor Model' by Paul Bennett

'A Practical Guide to Prison Injury Claims' by Malcolm Johnson

'A Practical Guide to Advising Clients at the Police Station' by Colin Stephen McKeown-Beaumont

'A Practical Guide to Antisocial Behaviour Injunctions – Second Edition' by Iain Wightwick

'Practical Mediation: A Guide for Mediators, Advocates, Advisers, Lawyers, and Students in Civil, Commercial, Business, Property, Workplace, and Employment Cases' by Jonathan Dingle with John Sephton

'The Mini-Pupillage Workbook' by David Boyle

'A Practical Guide to Crofting Law' by Brian Inkster

'A Practical Guide to the Law of Domain Names and Cybersquatting' by Andrew Clemson

'A Practical Guide to the Law of Gender Pay Gap Reporting' by Harini Iyengar

'NHS Whistleblowing and the Law' by Joseph England

'Employment Law and the Gig Economy' by Nigel Mackay & Annie Powell

'A Practical Guide to Noise Induced Hearing Loss (NIHL) Claims' by Andrew Mckie, Ian Skeate, Gareth McAloon

'An Introduction to Beauty Negligence Claims – A Practical Guide for the Personal Injury Practitioner' by Greg Almond

'Intercompany Agreements for Transfer Pricing Compliance' by Paul Sutton

'Zen and the Art of Mediation' by Martin Plowman

'A Practical Guide to Adoption for Family Lawyers' by Graham Pegg

www.ingramcontent.com/pod-product-compliance
Lightning Source LLC
LaVergne TN
LVHW022104200926
848481LV00003B/1061